Stop Paying Your Credit Cards

Obtain Credit Card Debt Forgiveness
Volume 1
---Second Edition---

Arthur V. Prosper

COPYRIGHT©2016 BY ARTHUR V. PROSPER * A-TEAM PUBLISHING GROUP * PO BOX 153 * PINEBROOK, NEW JERSEY 07058

COPYRIGHT AND TRADEMARK OWNERSHIP

All rights reserved. No part of this publication may be reproduced, stored in a retrieval system or transmitted by any means, electronic, mechanical, photocopying, recording, scanning or otherwise except as permitted under Section 107 or 108 of the 1976 United States Copyright Act, without the prior permission of the author and publisher.

Please be aware that any unauthorized use of the contents contained herein violates copyright laws, trademark laws, the laws of privacy and publicity, and/or other regulations and statutes. All text, images and other materials provided herein are owned by **Arthur V. Prosper** unless otherwise attributed to third parties. None of the content on these materials may be copied, reproduced, distributed, downloaded, displayed, or transmitted in any form without the prior written permission of **Arthur V. Prosper**, the legal copyright owner. However, you may copy, reproduce, distribute, download, display, or transmit the content of the materials for personal, non-commercial use provided that full attribution and citation to **Arthur V. Prosper** is included and the content is not modified, and you retain all copyright and other proprietary notices contained in the content. The permission stated above is automatically rescinded if you breach any of these terms or conditions. If permission is rescinded or denied, you must immediately destroy any downloaded and/or printed content.

FBI Anti-Piracy Warning: The unauthorized reproduction or distribution of a copyrighted work is illegal. Criminal copyright infringement, including infringement without monetary gain, is investigated by the FBI and is punishable by up to five years in federal prison and a fine of $250,000.

PAPERBACK ISBN: 978-1976842764
Imprint: Independently published by:
A-Team, PO Box 153, Pinebrook, NJ 07058
Cover Design by: Kristjan Victorino
Printed in the United States
Author's Email Address: arthurvprosper@gmail.com

Also by Arthur V. Prosper

The Simplest Path to Wealth: Turn $50,000 into $3.3 Million

DEBT FORGIVENESS Volume 2 WHEN CREDITORS DECIDE TO SUE

Dynamic Budgeting Techniques: Cut your expenses in half and double your income

How Much Federal Income Tax Will I Pay in 2018? The New Tax Law's winners and losers

The Six Million Dollar Retiree: Your roadmap to a six million dollar retirement nest egg

Living Rich & Loving It: Your guide to a rich, happy, healthy, simple and balanced life

Copyright©2016 by Arthur V. Prosper

DISCLAIMER

Notice: The information contained in this book is provided to you "AS IS" and does not constitute legal advice. All sample forms are for educational purposes only. We make no claims, promises or guarantees about the accuracy, completeness, or any specific result from the use of the contents or adequacy of the information contained in this book. Information contained in this book should not be used as substitute for obtaining legal advice from an attorney licensed or authorized to practice in your jurisdiction. The author is not a lawyer. No warranties are made regarding the suitability of this book. This book contains an accumulation of information based on the personal experience of the author. Prior results do not guarantee a similar outcome.

All rights reserved. No part of this book may be reproduced by any means without prior permission from the author.

****

If you have questions or comments, visit the author's website at: http://Arthur V. Prosper.com/

Contents

About the Author 5
Preface to the Second Edition 6
Introduction 9
Common Fallacies of Debt Settlement 17
Stop Paying Your Credit Cards! 23
What will the creditors do when you stop paying? 25
What will happen if you ignore the Creditor's collection Measures? 31
Collection Timeline If You Just Stop Paying 34
Write the Letter or Face a Lawsuit 37
My Personal Experience 41
Your Tax on Cancelled Debt 45
DO'S AND DONT'S of Credit Card Debt Negotiation 46
When the Credit Card Company Refuses to Negotiate 48
Validation of Debt, Cease and Desist Letter-Sample 50
WRITE THIS LETTER 58
Release - Sample 61
Counter Settlement Letter 62
Creditors' request for financial information 69
Sample timeline of the collection process 71
CONCLUSION-Volume 1 79
Living Rich and Loving It: 84
More about the Author 88
Supplemental Disclaimer 88
Copyright and Trademark Ownership 89

About the Author

Arthur V. Prosper is a freelance writer, author and columnist with 30 years of market experience. He writes articles about the markets and finance under the header "DidoSphere, DidoSpin and Vox Populi". He is the author of several published articles in business, politics, sports and entertainment including: How We Got Here, Market Crash of 2008, Housing Bubble, The Obama Recession, Bank Stress Tests & Other Terms, Scrap Mark to Market Valuation, Recession Over, The Labyrinth of Obamacare, Bush-Obama Recession, No Different From the Rest, A Tale of Two States, NJ & VA, SEC's Case vs. GS&CO., Weak, Most Experts Agree, PIIGS: Too Big to Fail, What Causes Stock Market Fluctuations, Sluggish Recovery, Good for Investors, QE2=Printing Money, Stock Market Investors, Fasten Your Seatbelt, No Double Dip Recession, 10% Unemployment Rate, Not Enough to Derail Recovery

Preface to the Second Edition

This is the Second Edition of the book, ***"Stop Paying Your Credit Cards - Obtain Credit Card Debt Forgiveness, Volume 1"***. This Second Edition was published on July 10, 2018.

The First Edition, published on December 29, 2015 covered the basic steps you should take if you cannot pay your credit cards anymore because of financial difficulties. The First Edition concentrated on negotiation, with writing and mailing ***"The Letter"*** as the first step. The step by step strategy discussed in the first edition became so effective for those who followed it that some credit card company collectors have come to affectionately refer to ***"The Letter"*** as "the kiss of debt". I learned this from a relative who works for Chase Credit Card customer service. She said that when someone receives a certified mail which seems to have a cut up credit card inside, before even opening the envelope, they quip, "Uh oh another one of those kiss of debt letters. We might as well write it off…" or "oh sh**, another one. Might as well send it to the lawyer now." The success of the ***"The Letter"*** has prompted some credit card company's inside collectors to make a decision quicker: to accept the settlement offer, make a counter-offer or refer the matter to a local collection attorney. When a collection attorney comes to the realization that "this" is not an easy case, that he still will not collect any money from you even if he files a civil suit, he will either abandon the case, accept your offer or make a counter-offer.

This Second Edition incorporates feedback received from readers by private email or as comments in my website, didoSphere.com. Most of the readers' comments are about the success they've accomplished by following the strategy in this book. A few expressed disappointment that ***The Letter*** did not work. Apparently, these readers thought success comes immediately after mailing **The Letter** and doing nothing else. They were not willing to follow through the subsequent procedures defined in this book. The step by step system was too much work for these readers, and they were oblivious to the fact that the likely outcome by following the procedures is to get rid of an oppressive credit card debt. I discovered that typing letters and sending them by certified mail presents a great difficulty to many of my readers. They prefer making telephone calls which will not accomplish anything. Writing letters and creating a trail is more effective in my experience and in the experience of over 100 of my readers.

Still, some readers reported of some pitfalls and traps they encountered after the credit card company's collection attorney filed suit. Since the burden of proof is on the credit card company to come up with evidence of the existence of a contract between you and them, lately credit card company lawyers have been coming up with new tricks and mumbo jumbo designed to confuse credit card holders who have decided to fight their law suits. One creative trick one collection lawyer played on one of my readers is to claim that: "I am not a collector, therefore I am not subject to the FDCPA rules" (see Volume 2). Another one said, "We are willing to stop this lawsuit if you give us your bank account and list of your assets…" Yet another one, a credit card company lawyer threatened one of my readers to file charges against her for "fraud", for intentionally defrauding the credit card company by making huge purchases on credit and taking cash advances knowing she had no intention of paying them back. And finally one lawyer threatened to charge one of my readers with perjury if he does not admit that he owes the money. But this reader learned enough from my books so as not to get intimidated by empty threats. Read how my reader dealt with this big badass collection attorney in Volume 2, Chapter, "What really happens after creditor files suit?" Many of these new collector's tricks are incorporated in this Second Edition.

Most of my readers learned from this book what most collection attorneys already know: A credit card company's statement and a computer-generated card member's account agreement do not constitute a contract between the credit card company and the credit card holder. Collectors who file suits often succeed in collecting money from the credit card holder not by proving the existence of a contract and the breach of such contract by the credit card holder, but by admission of the credit card holder of the existence of a contract. Proving the existence of a contract is a monumental task for the credit card company so that they are forced to abandon the lawsuit if the credit card holder never admits the existence of a contract. For those of you readers who think "not admitting you have a credit card account and that the balance is correct" (…or "not admitting to your debt") is somewhat dishonest, cunning and deceitful, please read my side of the argument in Chapter, **"Conclusion"** and discover what the credit card companies are all about.

Finally, most important of all, in this Second Edition, ***The Letter*** was revised to keep up with the times to make it more effective than before.

Introduction

I want to thank you for purchasing the book, ***"Stop Paying Your Credit Cards - Obtain Credit Card Debt Forgiveness, Volume 1"***. If this book is worthy of your praise, your positive review would be much appreciated.

What this book IS about:
      This book is about negotiating forgiveness for your credit card debt by writing your creditor one simple negotiation letter, and what to do if the creditor refuses to negotiate. If you owe money on your credit cards and you cannot make payments anymore because of financial difficulty, this book is for you. If you follow what I did, you may succeed in getting your creditors to forgive 85% to 95% of what you owe. It is not up to the credit card company to dictate the amount of settlement they are willing to accept. The settlement they have to accept is the amount you say you can afford to pay.

What this book is NOT about:
-Dave Ramsey or Suze Orman type financial advice
-Credit Repair
-Budgeting
-Motivation, Positive Thinking, Karma
-Financial Planning
-Economics, finance, banking, history lessons
-Credit Counseling
-Behavior modification, lifestyle change
-Debt Management
-Bankruptcy
-Numbers, Statistics and Analyses
-Interpretation of credit scores or credit report
-Analysis of why you overspend

-Discussion of things you already know such as, "what is a credit card?", "you and your credit cards have been in a relationship...", "when you take a loan, the lender charges you interest", "credit card interests are high", "how much you owe", "why you owe so much", "why you can't save", "diseases caused by mental stress", etc., etc.

****

If you need advice on budgeting, personal money management, stress-free investing, funding college education and retirement planning, download the author's new cradle to grave, guide-to-life book, ***Living Rich and Loving It"*,*

https://www.amazon.com/Living-Rich-Loving-healthy-balanced-ebook/dp/B01GORIB4Y/ref=sr_1_3?s=digital-text&ie=UTF8&qid=1465482641&sr=1-3&keywords=Arthur V. Prosper

- **You will learn how to:**
  - **Create a simple budget you can live with**
  - **Maximize contributions to your retirement account**
  - **Never lose money in the stock market**
  - **Predict the start and the end of a recession**
  - **Buy your principal residence**
  - **Choose between a traditional 401k and a Roth 401k**
  - **Accumulate over $3 million in your retirement account**
  - **Calculate the amount of life insurance you need**

- Determine the right time to start collecting social security
- Maximize your Social Security benefits
- Pay for long-term care
- Qualify for Medicaid
- Preserve your lifetime savings
- Manage emergencies without "an emergency fund"
- Find the job you love
- Fund your children's college education
- Find creative ways to increase your income
- Create a document storage and retrieval system
- Implement a personal time management system
- Store and safeguard strong passwords
- Plan for retirement
- Locate the best places to retire
- Spend your leisure time wisely
- Stay healthy and fit
- Live a rich, happy and healthy life

****

I owed over $100,000 in credit card debt and the debt was hurting my life. I kept borrowing on my credit cards because I lost my job and the job I found after a one year job search only paid half of what I used to make. To make matters worse two of my family members whom I am responsible for had health issues and the insurance deductibles and co-pays depleted our family's emergency fund. I was stressed out and was having trouble sleeping at night thinking how long my ever-increasing debt would continue to gnaw at me. I sat down in front of my computer and created an excel amortization schedule. If I only made the minimum payments and do not borrow anymore, with compounding interest of 25% APR, I will still owe a substantial amount of money after many years of making minimum monthly payments. The interest alone would cost me close to $100,000. But the bottom line was, I no longer had enough money in my budget to keep making even the minimum monthly payments.

It took a year of trial and error, of countless hours on the phone and writing meaningless letters, most of which I copied from various articles and websites in the internet before I saw the light at the end of the tunnel. None of the free advice and letters in the internet applied to me because the truth is I was not insolvent. I had a steady job, owned personal properties, a 401k account with an $80,000 balance and a large equity on my principal residence. I could have liquidated my assets, paid off my $100,000 credit card debt and still be left with a small amount of cash in the end. In reality I did not qualify for bankruptcy protection. But because of the health issues, selling the house at that time and uprooting the entire family from a 4-bedroom house in a nice and safe neighborhood into a 2-bedroom apartment in a "not-so-nice" neighborhood would have been devastating. The stress of the move alone could have made the medical problems a lot worse.

I was tempted to follow the advice I read on the internet to simply stop making payments and let the credit card companies sue me, let them secure a judgment against me, put a lien on my properties and/or garnish my wages---let the chips fall where they may so to speak. It is a good thing I did not heed the foolish advice because the cost of hiring a lawyer to answer lawsuits and spending my time going to court could have cost me a lot more money than just paying the balance. If you have nothing to lose, then there is nothing the creditors can take away from you. But my case was different. I kept on thinking that there must be a better way. How about begging the credit card companies to reduce what I owe? Is that possible? I wrote my creditors one letter after another until I finally came up with *The Letter* that uniformly worked in negotiating down my debt with my credit card providers. After mailing *The Letter* to the credit card companies, I received a reply from a collection agency representing one of them offering to accept 50% of what I owe as full payment of my debt. That was not good enough for me so I countered with 5%. After a brief back and forth negotiation, we finally agreed on 10% of the original amount as full and final settlement of my balance. Considering I had not paid them for a year, I accumulated a little cash, so I was happy to grab the offer. I had five credit cards with large balances and *The Letter* worked satisfactorily on four of the accounts. I settled the other 3 accounts for between 5% and 15% from money I borrowed on my 401k account at 5% per APR interest…a lot less than the 28% the credit card companies were charging me. The last hold-out, surprisingly the account with the smallest balance at $13,000 chose to take me to arbitration. This negotiation-resistant creditor perceived that they might collect more money from me that way but they were wrong. More of that in Volume 2. I was surprised that not one of the 4 creditors even referred to the contents of *The Letter* or attempted to verify what I had written in the letter. They went right into negotiation mode. Apparently the letter was composed in such a way as to paint a clear picture to convince my creditors that it is in their best interest to take what they can get. It had to be composed that way because unlike other debtors who have nothing to lose, I had a lot to lose. Therefore, *The Letter* aims to convey this message to the creditors: "Take my final settlement offer or sue me. But if you sue me, you will lose". For those of you who think this strategy is somewhat dishonest, cunning and deceitful please read my side of the argument in the chapter entitled "Conclusion – Volume 1".

These are the steps I followed: 1) Write *The Letter*, 2) stop making payments, 3) wait 30 days for a reply, 4) negotiate a lower amount if the creditor wants more than 15%, 5) write up with 2 or 3 follow up letters if the creditor is not replying or is refusing to come down to 15% or lower, 6) write a Validation of

Debt, Cease and Desist Letter, 7) write letters to challenge CC Company's validation of debt (see these letters under Chapter "Validation of Debt, Cease and Desist"), 8) reply to the creditor's Complaint if you get sued, 9) mail the Plaintiff a Request for Production of Documents, Admissions and Interrogatories, 10) file a Motion for Summary Judgment.

Steps 6 to 10 are explained in more detail in Volume 2 of this series.

An actual "offer letter" from one of my credit card providers is shown below after I had countered their 50% offer of settlement with 5%. Confidential and sensitive information was changed to protect the privacy of all concerned:

****

Cardmember Services
P.O. Box 15222
Wilmington, DE 19850-5298
1-866-252-5334
KY
1-800-955-8799

Arthur V. Prosper
Address
City, State, Zip

September 06, 2012

Action Needed: **Act now to settle your account for $3,017.16**

Your account ending in 3770

Dear Arthur V. Prosper:

We want to work with you to resolve your delinquent account, so we'd like to offer you a settlement. Your current account balance is $30,171.60; however we'll accept payment of $3,017.16 to settle the account and stop further collection activities. You'll save $27,154.44.

You can accept this offer until 10/06/2012.

Here are your payment options
- Make one payment of $3,017.16 by 09/27/2012, or
- Make two payments of $1508.58 by 09/20/2012 and a second payment of $1508.58 by 10/18/2012.

Here's how to accept our offer
- Pay by phone by calling 1-866-252-5999, or
- Pay by mail by sending a check or money order payable to Card Member Services. Write your account number in the memo field and mail it to:

Cardmember Services
PO Box 94222
Palatine, IL 60094-4014

We're here to help
If you have questions or want to make other payment arrangements, please call us at 1-866-252-5999. We're here Monday through Friday from 8 a.m. to 10 p.m. and Saturday from 8 a.m. to 5 p.m. Eastern Time.

Sincerely,

Customer Support Team

The IRS requires us to report canceled debts through Form 1099-C. We'll send you a copy of IRS Form 1099-C if we filed it to report your debt. If we settle this debt with you for less than the full outstanding balance, Cardmember Services may offer you less favorable terms in the future for some Cardmember Services products or services, or may deny your application. This is an attempt to collect a debt. Any information obtained will be used for that purpose. Cardmember Services is the owner of the account.

****

When I received the above offer, I decided that maybe it was time to accept the offer, although it was not the 5% I was hoping for. I issued a check for $3,017.16 and typed in the back of the check: "Encashment of this check releases maker of any and all liabilities for cc account ****3770".

Common Fallacies of Debt Settlement

In the article "8 Myths about Settling Credit Card Debt", authors Sally Herigstad and Karen Haywood Queen wrote, "That anyone can get their credit card balance cut in half for any reason, is a myth". "Both creditors and legitimate debt settlement companies screen clients to ensure their hardship meets underwriting criteria", says Brian Tawney, co-legislative director and executive board member of the American Fair Credit Council and counsel for Clear One Advantage debt settlement company. "Debt settlement is for hardships such as a temporary job loss, divorce or medical problems", Tawney says. ""Often our client's situation results from unemployment, underemployment, divorce, death, medical issues and for some, overspending,"" he says.

My Comment: The fact is that there is NO underwriting criteria or screening done by the creditor to ascertain that a delinquent debtor is a genuine hardship case. They don't care. They just want their money back. The debt settlement agency may do some screening to find out if your cash flow would allow for payment of their fee as well as to set aside a certain amount of savings each month to use as a settlement offer to the creditor as the savings builds up. If you don't make enough, the agency will not take your case. The debt settlement companies only take the easy cases and this is fair because they are in business to make a profit. If you have too much money and have a good positive cash flow but are demanding too much of a discount, say 80% reduction of your debt, the agency will not take your case because they will spend an excessive amount of time pleading your case with your creditors. Debt settlement agencies are not well known for their success in negotiating 5% to 20% settlements for their clients. It is more like 50% which you yourself can negotiate without too much effort.

The creditors' collection efforts are not contingent upon a debtor's hardship or type of hardship. In essence the credit card company does not care about you and your personal problems. They just want their money back or alternatively recover as much as they can from you, the debtor. Creditors are no more merciful and forgiving towards the unemployed and divorcees than towards over spenders. The amount of debt a creditor is willing to cancel or forgive is the amount they think they CANNOT collect from that debtor. If they perceive they can collect 100% of the debt, they will not be too willing to forgive even a dollar of that debt. They do not care if you got divorced, lost your job or got sick. The credit card company is a business not a welfare agency so the reason for your default is not a big factor in negotiating a settlement with you. If they think or perceive that they can collect money from you because you have the means, they will employ various collection tactics to continue to hound you. If collecting the debt becomes difficult for them and they find themselves spending an inordinate amount of time and resources for the amount of money you owe, they will bail out, negotiate a settlement with you or sell your debt to a junk debt buyer for pennies on the dollar. Why not try to settle with them for 5 cents on the dollar? They may be willing to take what they can get at this particular point.

In the article "8 Myths About Settling Credit Card Debt" it sounds like the debt settlement company will screen the debtor first after which they will make a determination on whether or not to accept the case, i.e. do you make enough money to pay the creditor as well as the debt settlement agency? If the debt settlement agency determines your offer to be too low, they will probably reject it and say, "C'mon, you make more than enough to offer a little bit more. The creditor will never accept this offer…" In this respect, the debt settlement company is the de facto agent of the credit card company because you cannot just walk into their office and say, "I can only afford to pay 10% of my debt". Their reply will probably be: "WE will make the determination how much you can afford to pay. The credit card company will not accept your offer because it is too low". They will screen you first to find out the maximum they can squeeze out of you before taking your case. My system of requesting debt forgiveness is simpler. You put your fate in your own hands by writing *The Letter* shown at the end of this book, then follow the step by step procedure if they ignore *The Letter*.

Other quotes from the same article are shown below, followed by my comments:

Ken Clark, author of The Complete Idiot's Guide to Getting out of Debt: "So many people are trying to get their balances reduced, you call and try to negotiate a balance, and it's "Get in line." The card company's attitude may be, "Yeah, you and everybody else"".

My Comment: That's because you called to negotiate instead of writing *The Letter* shown at the end of this book. Trust me there aren't that many accounts in default as a percentage of the whole or our banking system would collapse. If you write *The Letter* shown at the end of this book, the creditor will put you at the front of the line.

Brian Tawney, Director of Clear One Advantage: "Based on experience negotiating with creditors, debt settlement companies know what percentage of debt owed each creditor is likely to agree to. We use an algorithm that considers 140 different variables and tells us the accounts that have the highest opportunity to settle at any given time. We negotiate in bulk. We can negotiate thousands of cases and get a better settlement for everyone."

My Comment: I do not know what kind of system or algorithm this debt settlement agency is referring to but it sounds like if you approach them they will first make a pre-determination of the amount of debt you should ask the creditor to forgive. The explanation of their system makes sense because they cannot possibly have enough employees to negotiate individually for each client. Negotiation takes time and the agency is in business to make money so they do not necessarily have the debtor's best interest in mind. If you tell them "I can only pay 5% of the balance", their reply will probably be, "the creditor will never accept it. Your algorithm says you can afford 33%". The credit card companies know and trust these debt settlement agencies, the reputable ones and appreciate the fact that they do the bargaining for them by nailing the maximum amount a delinquent debtor can pay. Oftentimes the credit card company will agree to delay the filing of a suit against a delinquent debtor who is a client of a reputable debt settlement agency that they've had the experience to work with. But I like my system better. It is not that complicated. You write the letter shown at the end of this book which begs creditors to forgive 85% to 95% of your debt. The creditors can take it or leave it. If they take it, you win. If they leave it, they lose.

Sally Herigstad and Karen Haywood Queen: "You always have options. For example, if you lose your job and you call your credit card company, they may give you "forbearance" -- in other words, they may allow you to make smaller payments or no payments at all for a time (you'll still be charged interest, however)".

My Comment: If you follow the aforementioned advice, your debt will continue to increase due to the huge interest added each month. In addition, the creditor may add late fees and penalties. The interest will convert to a "penalty interest rate" which can become as high as 35% APR. If you continue to make smaller payments they will assume they can jack up your debt and they will continue to receive your smaller payments over a longer period of time until paid in full which could be 30 years. The clock on the statute of limitation for your debt will not start ticking until you stop making payments. In some states, the collector only has 3 years to collect from the time the debtor stops making payments. After the statute of limitation runs out, the debt is time-barred, i.e. they lose their legal right to collect the debt. Therefore, continuing to make small payments will ensure that the creditor continues to maintain its legal claim against you. Making smaller payments even if the creditor agrees to it is really a bad idea. Just write *The Letter* shown at the end of this book and stop paying altogether. The bottom line is: Your creditors will not negotiate with you as long as you are making payments even if those payments are less than the minimum amount shown on your statement.

Here is one bankruptcy attorney's opinion about debt negotiation:

Greg Gouner, a bankruptcy lawyer in Baton Rouge, prefers filing for bankruptcy instead of negotiating a settlement for his clients: "I see my clients getting slammed with huge judgments and garnished for years. Bankruptcy is often the best route out of the jungle. My office has discharged millions in debt over the last 21 years. Debtors usually get a very fair shake in court. I understand if you want to take the hard line approach of "Sue Me." But I don't find most unrepresented people fare well in the legal system. I don't recommend debt settlement agencies. We have also beat back collection efforts in the court system and regularly represent folks who dispute debt. We are frequently successful with this, but it is harder than it sounds. When the chips are down, bankruptcy is a solution to consider".

My Comment: This lawyer sounds like the attorney I hired, see the section, "My Personal Experience". Of course it takes him less time to file bankruptcy papers for his clients than to negotiate individually for them. He has a bankruptcy template that his clerk simply fills out and files in court for his client and, voila, the client is bankrupt. Yes I agree that it is time consuming to negotiate on behalf of individual clients but bankruptcy is the last resort. But if you negotiate, you better do it right. These are the steps to follow: 1) Write *The Letter*, 2) stop making payments, 3) wait 30 days for a reply, 4) negotiate a lower amount than proposed by the creditor, 5) write up to 3 follow up letters if there is no reply from the creditor, 6) write a Validation of Debt, Cease and Desist Letter, 7) challenge the validation of debt documents sent by the creditor, 8) reply to the creditor's complaint if you get sued (See volume 2 of this series), 9) send the Plaintiff a Request for Production of Documents, Admissions and Interrogatories, 10) File a summary judgment against creditor. Use the creditor's failure to provide debt validation as an affirmative answer to creditor's complaint. Avoid bankruptcy if you can. Furthermore, many credit card debtors may not be insolvent, as in my case, hence under the law do not qualify for bankruptcy protection. I had a large equity in my principal residence which I was able to protect and preserve by going through and succeeding in the process of negotiating a settlement with my creditors on my own. Filing for bankruptcy is very stressful. It may include having to sell your house and other assets at the most inopportune moment to pay creditors' claims. Taking the hard line approach and telling the creditor to sue you is not a good idea either unless you know what you are doing and your endgame is clear. How will you answer the complaint when they do sue you? How will you negotiate with them at that point when they have the upper hand? It is much better to negotiate with your creditor before they even think of filing a lawsuit. *The Letter* shown towards the end of this book can convince them that your offer is the best they can hope for to recover any money from you and that rejection of your offer can cost them a lot of money in collection and legal fees. However, I still say you will do very well representing yourself in court if you follow what I did when one of my creditors refused to negotiate and decided to sue me instead. They received nothing from me and it only cost them a lot of money in legal fees. Read the book, "Debt Forgiveness Volume 2, When Creditors Decide to Sue", https://www.amazon.com/DEBT-FORGIVENESS-WHEN-CREDITORS-DECIDE-ebook/dp/B01ACTBTIU/ref=sr_1_7?s=digital-text&ie=UTF8&qid=1479931823&sr=1-7&keywords=Arthur V. Prosper#reader_B01ACTBTIU

Stop Paying Your Credit Cards!

Whether you owe $100,000 or only $10,000 on your credit cards, stop paying them if you are no longer able to make payments. Maintaining your sanity, putting food on the table, keeping the lights on, paying the rent or mortgage, paying for medical expenses and keeping up with your health insurance premiums are more important than continuing to make payments you cannot afford to make. You can negotiate a settlement of your credit card balance on your own for a fraction of what you owe. It is hard to imagine that such a monumental goal can be anything but next to impossible to achieve, but the truth is it is quite simple if you do the same thing I did. There is a trick to it and you have only one chance of doing it right. Any mistake in your initial communication with the credit provider, collector or collection attorney may prove to be irreparable. Your creditor will be able to determine from the tone and wording of your letter how much time and effort they will have to expend in collecting your debt. In addition, if you are not careful with the wording of your letter, you may inadvertently make unintended admissions such as admitting to your debt, to the interest rate you are being charged, to late fees, to a higher interest rate as soon as you miss a payment, to waiving your right to a jury trial, to settling disputes through arbitration, even to waiving your right to sue or counter sue your creditor. This initial communication must be in the form of a letter that must be sent by certified mail. Never communicate verbally by phone. Most credit card company collectors routinely record conversations with debtors, then find a way to show that you agreed to something you did not. They will get you to say the word "yes" and---wham!---you just admitted you owe the balance. Send a letter. *The Letter* you should use is shown at the end of this book. The alternative is to stop making payments, get sued, and hire a lawyer to defend the lawsuit or let the credit card companies obtain a judgment against you, garnish your wages and/or put a lien on your assets. This will cost you a lot more in the end.

What will the creditors do when you stop paying?

You should be aware of the things that are likely to happen the moment you miss the minimum payment on your credit card account. Most credit card companies are owned by banks and they are no different than other businesses that have to manage risk vs. benefit as part of their daily routine. As soon as you miss your minimum monthly payment, the games will begin.

The fact that they granted you credit without any collateral is proof that at the time, you were a good credit risk to them. Unsecured loans are very risky for creditors. They were so anxious to make money on you that the likelihood is that they did not even ask you to sign a credit card application agreement which is a positive proof of the existence of a contract. Every personal situation can change so if at any given time you become a bad risk, just like any other business, they have to assess how much they can collect from you and allocate the appropriate amount of time, effort and money in collecting your debt. In many cases, if your balance is small, say under $5000 they may decide it is not worth pursuing and they may just sell your debt to a collection agency. Chances are the creditors' in-house collectors or their collection agency will continue to call you, send regular reminders and report you to credit reporting agencies but will never actually file a lawsuit against you. They may just write off your balance as a bad debt and send you an IRS Form 1099-C for the amount they wrote off, see the chapter, "Your Tax on Cancelled Debt". Consumer debts have a nuisance value and when I managed the collections department of a large retailer, we did not bother filing suits on small claims, say amounts of $5000 or less because the time and effort spent in the filing of a suit, applying for a judgment and writ of garnishment, etc., cannot be justified by the amount of debt. However, lately creditors have wised up and made deals with local attorneys to file complaints in bulk against multiple delinquent debtors. It is not uncommon nowadays, if you sit in a courtroom of a small claims judge, to hear cases after cases being called where one common Plaintiff, (presumably a credit card provider) is suing many different defendants (presumably debtors) at the same time. For example cases called one after the other this way: HSBC vs. Smith, HSBC vs. Jones, HSBC vs. Williams, HSBC vs. Brown, etc. etc. For me this is proof that the credit card companies have found a cost effective way of obtaining default judgments and collecting on the judgments against debtors who owe smaller amounts, i.e. $5000 or less. It is more cost effective for a creditor to contract with a local attorney to try 10 cases at once than just one at a time. If five of the defendants do not show up, he can quickly file motions for default judgments right there and then. And for those defendant/debtors who show up for the hearing, he can take the hardline. In all likelihood not only will he demand the entire balance, he may demand that the debtor pay his legal fees. And this can all take place in a short period of 3 hours or less. The potential for collecting $50,000 for a half day work where the lawyer's fee is probably 1/3 of what he can collect plus expenses is not bad. Therefore, whatever the amount of your debt, it is in your best interest to respond in writing to collection calls and dunning letters to let the collectors know they cannot easily obtain a judgment against you. Various letters and exhibits are shown in this book to serve as outlines and guide. The strategy in this book requires that you reply to collection letters to establish your defense in case you get sued. However, if writing letters will cause you hardship and stress, then the strategy in this book is not for you. You must be willing and able to put in the time and effort to reply to the creditor/collector by certified mail in order to solidify your defense in the event the creditor/collector decides to file a civil suit against you. Maybe they will never put your case into litigation, but prepare for the worst and hope for the best.

Bad debts are a built in expense into the bank's financial statements and their profit margins are still some of the highest in any industry so don't feel sorry for them if they can only collect 25%, 10% or 5% of what you owe them. They still make huge profits and their officers earn millions of dollars in bonuses each year. The bad debts they charge off are business deductions on their company's income tax returns.

In the early stages of the collection process, the credit card companies have a cheap and effective way of dealing with debtors as soon as they miss a payment. They will employ soft-tactics and try to appear helpful. It can be described as psychological warfare but it works and they do not have to spend too much time, effort and resources to employ it. In fact their computers do it with little human intervention. We are talking about the usual collection tricks, robo calls, computer generated dunning letters, statements, reminders and other more sophisticated collection letters designed to be sympathetic at first but then work their way into scaring the debtor, such as adding late fees and collection charges to your balance. Seeing an additional $500 of late fees and collection charges being added to your statement each month can take a toll on your mental health. Other collection tricks that I personally experienced include collectors' phone messages 2 to 3 times a day which appear to be automated voice recordings from a male collector with a deep voice saying, "THIS IS MR. GOLDSTEIN. THIS IS NOT A SOLICITATION. THIS IS IMPORTANT. WE WANT TO TALK TO YOU ABOUT YOUR DELINQUENT ACCOUNT....." The voice was so creepy it gave me nightmares. Most of these collection techniques are effective. They are intimidating, threatening, can cause stress and can keep the debtor awake at night just like what they did to me.

If you are only paying the minimum amount on your account, you already know that interest can add up quickly. How much more if you are several months behind on your payments. An enormous amount of interest will keep getting added to your balance each month. If you default on one of your credit cards, your interest rate may convert to a penalty rate of 30% to 35% and the interest rates on other cards you own might go up too. In addition, you may have unwittingly agreed to pay additional late fees in addition to collection charges when you signed up and the credit card company can keep adding these charges to your account until such time that your account is current again. You may receive a letter urging you to make at least the minimum payment or you will be reported to Credit Reporting Agencies. These agencies are so powerful that they might as well be called Credit Gods. Most creditors rely on the information these agencies report which can affect whether you can get a loan and how much interest you have to pay to borrow money. How they acquired so much power is discussed in Volume 3 of this series. Negative information about a debtor in the Credit Reporting Agencies' files is very difficult to correct. There are recommended steps in the Federal Trade Commission's website on how to correct errors but the steps are painstaking. Although the reporting agency is required by law to reply to your request to correct erroneous information, there is nothing in the law that states that you, the debtor are correct and the creditor is wrong. It is easy enough and cost effective for a creditor to say "what we reported is accurate". However, this is not the time to worry about your credit scores. When times are rough, you make a choice: continue paying your credit cards or put food on the table. For now, let them report you, control your destiny and get rid of your credit card debts first, worry about your FICO credit scores later. Repairing your credit is discussed in more detail in Volume 2 of this series and there is a way to rebuild your FICO credit scores by following a few simple steps, especially if your creditor failed to provide the information demanded on your Validation of Debt letter. For now your family is your top priority. Take care of your loved ones first by getting rid of your huge debt before worrying about your credit scores. A credit card debt free life will provide you and your family with a better

chance for a brighter future. Yes, initially your FICO credit scores will go down to 600 after your debts are "settled", "forgiven" or "charged off" which happened in my case. Within a year of having my credit card debts written off (or forgiven), I decided to refinance my home mortgage loan because of the favorable rates. Of course the cancelled debts appeared on my credit reports as "charge-off" and the bank I am refinancing with asked for an explanation. I told the bank that the amounts the creditors charged off were unverified debts and sent them copies of the following documents: 1) Validation of Debt Requests for which I never received a reply, 2) a copy of the Court Judgment, the dismissal with prejudice of the Complaint of the credit card company that decided to sue me, 3) copies of my letters to the IRS disputing the creditors' Forms 1099-C, requesting the IRS to obtain verification of debt from the creditors pursuant to U.S. Code-Title 26 Section 6201(d) for which I never received a reply (the letter to the IRS is in Volume 2 of this series). Lo and behold, the bank approved my refinancing application for a 15-year fixed mortgage at a 2.85% APR. As I kept making my monthly mortgage payments, my FICO scores kept going up. See the topic, **How to Mitigate Negative Credit Report** in volume 2, **Debt Forgiveness, Volume 2: When Creditors Decide to Sue,**
https://www.amazon.com/DEBT-FORGIVENESS-Chapter-CREDITORS-DECIDE-ebook/dp/B01ACTBTIU/ref=pd_sbs_351_4?ie=UTF8&psc=1&refRID=GPVCVBC5R12HPRD4K7TP#nav-subnav

Yes, your creditors will continue their collection efforts by calling you perhaps more than once a day and you may receive a letter from an attorney or a collection agency threatening to file suit by a certain date if you do not make at least your minimum payment. These tactics are all so basic and too cost effective and designed to scare you into resuming your payments. If you make small payments, less than the required minimum, this game can continue indefinitely but to your detriment. Your debt will continue to increase due to the huge interest added each month. Your credit score will keep going down. But the worst part about continuing to make small payments is that it could be construed as an admission of your alleged debt, including any amount they add to your balance that you may not have agreed to such as late fees, penalties and collection charges. As previously discussed, the clock on the statute of limitation will not start ticking until you stop making payments completely.

What will happen if you ignore the Creditor's collection Measures?

If you ignore the creditor's collection efforts, you can get sued, lose a judgment and be forced to pay your creditor. On the other hand, if you write your creditor a simple letter, your credit card problems could all be solved. The choice could not be easier. *The Letter* you should write is shown at the end of this book. If you do not have any recent major purchase my advice is to write *The Letter* before your default (before missing a payment). Do not wait 90 to 180 days as many credit advisors recommend. I guess the rationale for waiting 90 days or more is to drive the point to your creditors that you are seriously not going to make any payments anymore. But you should also be aware that if you racked up charges only recently for a major purchase such as for a dining room set or for a major expense such as for an expensive European vacation, an astute collector may threaten to bring charges against you for fraud, i.e. borrowing money knowing you have no intention of paying it back. A judgment for fraud awarded against a debtor cannot be discharged in bankruptcy so you have to be careful. If this is the case with you, my advice is to continue making the minimum payments in order to give the recent large charge time to age before going delinquent. If you have been delinquent for a long time, by all means send *The Letter* by certified mail immediately. The sooner you communicate your intention to your creditor the better. That way, there is a better chance for a decision maker at the credit card company to negotiate with you before deciding to sell your debt to a junk debt collector or attorney which is what they do when the debt is neglected and gets too old which to the original creditor is around 6 months. Though they may mark your account "charged off" after 6 months, it does not mean it went away. It means they wrote it off their balance sheet and charged it off as a bad debt expense on their corporate income

tax return. Some creditors have "bad debt insurance". They will collect on the insurance only after they write off the debt. After they write it off they may still continue to collect your alleged debt on their own, assign your debt to a collection agency or collection attorney or sell your account to a debt collector for 10% to 15% of what you owe. From my experience, junk debt collectors and collection lawyers are a lot tougher and more annoying than credit card companies' in house collectors. ***If you or your spouse have accounts at the same bank that issued your credit cards, your accounts may be charged for what the bank will describe as "bad debt recovery charge".*** See Volume 2 for more information on this subject.
https://www.amazon.com/DEBT-FORGIVENESS-WHEN-CREDITORS-DECIDE-ebook/dp/B01ACTBTIU/ref=sr_1_2?ie=UTF8&qid=1490212136&sr=8-2&keywords=Arthur V. Prosper

  If you do nothing after you stop paying, and your balance is more than $5000, the creditor's next move would presumably be in the form of a "Final Notice" from a collection agency or from a local attorney threatening to file a lawsuit or an arbitration hearing by a particular date. If they do not receive a reply from you and they perceive that you have some assets and/or the ability to pay, they might assume that they have an easy path to obtaining a default judgment against you. Losing a lawsuit by default or by summary judgment is something you never want to happen. If a creditor wins a judgment against you, they can execute the judgment through the sheriff's office to get an order for garnishment of your salary or put a lien on your bank accounts and other assets such as your car, truck, boat, motorcycle or trailer. In Texas, a judgment cannot be filed as a lien on your homestead and your wages cannot be garnished. But in some states, a judgment against you will be recorded as an automatic lien on any real estate you own, whether a principal residence or investment properties. An order for garnishment of your wages can create a bad impression for you at your place of employment since your employer and some co-workers who may find out, may assume that you have money problems. A judgment against you can stay on your credit report for 7 years and can remain enforceable for 10 to 20 years depending on where you live. Different states have different laws. If you have no assets and are not presently working, do not make a mistake in thinking that you are free from the judgment. The creditor may lay low for now then decide to execute the judgment in the future, perhaps when they find out that you have newly acquired assets and are gainfully employed again. The Statute of limitation for debt collection is different from the life of a judgment that was granted in any competent Court. This is discussed in more detail in Volume 3 of this series. Bottom line is, if you have no job and no assets you might be tempted to simply stop paying and stop communicating with your creditors. They will report you to credit reporting agencies, may or may not file suit against you and then may or may not obtain a judgment against you. If you are nonchalant about it, consider what may happen in the future. The interest rate you have to pay in the future or whether or not anyone will even grant you a loan depends on your credit scores. In most states, a judgment against you may be recorded as a lien on properties you own or have interest in. If you buy real estate you will not be able to acquire a clean title until you have satisfied the judgment. Junk debt collectors, the bottom feeders, the bounty hunters for bad debts regularly go through public records in order to find unsatisfied judgments to collect. If yours happens to be the one they pick, the miserable collection game will start anew and you are back to square one.

Collection Timeline If You Just Stop Paying

The following is a sample timeline as to what may happen from the moment you stop paying your credit card completely, you do not write *THE LETTER* shown in that Chapter and you just don't do anything else:
- STOPPED PAYING YOUR CREDIT CARD ACCOUNT COMPLETELY.
- CC Company will send you a statement the following month with additional interests.
- CC Company will send you a statement a month later with added interests and possibly additional late fees.
- After 60 days, CC Company will send you a new statement with late fees and possibly additional interests computed at a higher rate (penalty interest) which can be as high as 35%. The CC's in house collector will keep calling you probably several times a day. The collector may even call you at your place of work.
- After 90 days, collection efforts usually intensify and the collector usually writes a letter or calls to inform you that your delinquency will be reported to credit reporting agencies. Collectors may also sound sympathetic and may give you the impression that they are willing to work with you by lowering your interest and your minimum payments. At this juncture, you may be tempted to accept their offer to pay a small amount out of fear especially since your balance keeps going up even though you have not been making additional purchases. It is psychological warfare at this point since you don't know the end game and your balance has probably increased by 12% since you first stopped paying. It will be a mistake to make even a very small payment because that can restart the collection clock and the collection attorney may use the resumption of payments as an admission of your debt.

- The intensified collection efforts will continue until the end of six months after your delinquency. At which time, the CC Company may choose to charge off your account so as to enable them to write off the debt as a bad debt which is a deductible expense on their corporate tax return. If they do this, they will report your debt as "charge off" to reporting agencies. They may refer your account to a local attorney for collection on a contingency basis or sell it outright to a junk debt collector for between 5% and 10% of the balance.
- The junk debt collector will restart the collection process and can make your life miserable. Some unscrupulous collectors may even violate a few FDCPA collection rules such as calling you before 8am and after 9pm, not disclosing that they are a debt collector, giving the impression that the collector is a lawyer and that you can be arrested if you do not pay your debt.
- A local attorney who may work for the CC Company for a fee or on contingency may initially send you just the casual pre-printed collection letters. After 60 to 90 days, if you do not reply, he may send you a FINAL NOTICE BEFORE SUIT. This final notice is usually sent by certified mail to impress upon you that this has become a serious matter.
- If the attorney does not receive a reply, he may actually file suit and you will receive a summons together with the Complaint. See the Chapter, Creditor's/Plaintiff's Complaint in Volume 2. The Complaint will include the attorney's fees and court filing fees. You generally have 30 days to reply to the Complaint in most jurisdictions.
- If you do not reply to the Complaint, the attorney will file a motion for default judgment and the judge may grant him that judgment.
- In most states, the attorney may be allowed to file a Writ of Garnishment or Writ of Execution to collect on the judgment and to direct your employer to garnish (deduct) a certain amount from your wages; the banks to turn over your money to satisfy the judgment; record a lien and seize or sell your properties

through a sheriff's sale. In most states, your primary residence (homestead) is exempt from execution but other states only have monetary limits on the homestead value that may be exempted from seizure.

If the CC Company wins a default judgment against you, it will be a bigger nightmare to go through a sheriff's sale for your non-exempt properties. If you follow the system, it is unlikely that the attorney will go through filing a civil suit against you because the letters in these two books will convey the message that you have the time, skill and inclination to answer and oppose the creditor's Complaint and that it will not be profitable for the attorney and the original creditor to go through with it.

Write the Letter or Face a Lawsuit

If you write *The Letter* shown at the end of this book, the creditor's next move will probably be an attempt to negotiate a settlement with you. In all likelihood you will receive a letter from the creditor like the one that follows:

"Dear Credit Card Holder:
We received your letter dated xx/xx/xx. We will accept $xx,xxx.xx (usually 50%) as full payment of your account but we must receive your payment by xx/xx/xx (date). If we do not receive your payment by this date, we will turn your account over to our collection attorney for further action."

If you receive such a letter, just say no. You are having financial difficulty and can only pay 5% as full settlement. It's a negotiation at this point. Send a counter-settlement letter. A sample is shown towards the end of this book. Remember, any letters you send out must be by certified mail. Do not accept any settlement without a release from any and all liabilities. If you accept a settlement without the release, it is not uncommon for the creditor or collector to sell or resell the amount you thought was forgiven to a junk debt collector for collection. The release is shown towards the end of this book. It should be stapled to *The Letter* for the convenience of the creditor, to make it easy for the creditor/collector to sign and send back to you. As an additional measure, on the memo section on the front of your check, type or print "Full Payment of Acct No. xxxx xxxx xxxx xxxx". On the back of the check, type or print, "Endorsement, acceptance, deposit, encashment of this check by payee, discharges payer from any and all liabilities to payee". When the creditor receives *The Letter* from you, they may get the impression that this case is more difficult to collect than others and that they may not collect anything at all even if they win a judgment against you. It may make them more inclined to negotiate in order to recover "something". For most creditors, taking legal action against a debtor is very risky. Suing costs a lot of money and most of them do not want to throw good money after bad. They may be willing to take what they can get at this point in the game.

If you don't do anything at all after Creditor sends you the aforementioned letter or you cannot come to an agreement with the creditor, then you are back to square one. The creditor's collector will keep calling you and keep sending you a few more collection letters and reminders and it can get worse from there. If you start receiving letters from a collection agency or an attorney, there is a great possibility that they have outsourced or sold your delinquent account to a collection agency or an attorney in your area. These are the bottom feeders who scoop up the crumbs from the bottom and probably bought your account from the original creditor for pennies on the dollar. Some collectors are so aggressive and so notorious for flagrant violations of some of the provisions of the Fair Debt Collection Practices Act (FDCPA) such as, 1) Contacting a third party who does not owe the debt, 2) Making false threats such as filing suit without the intention of doing so or threats of physical violence, 3) Making repeated phone calls at unreasonable times, 4) Contacting you at your place of business in clear violation of your employer's policy, 5) Using obscenity, racial slurs and insults, 5) Sending letters which appear to have come from a court, 6) Requesting post-dated checks with the intention to prosecute if they bounce, 7) Filing suit in courts far removed from your place of residence, 8) Impersonating an attorney or giving the impression that the collector is an attorney, 9) Using false claims to collect information about the debtor, such as pretending to be conducting a survey, 10) Threatening you with arrest if you do not pay the debt.

Some attorneys are also so aggressive that they can put your account into litigation immediately if you do not reply within the period of time they gave you. They think you are apt to negotiate more promptly and more submissively if you receive a summons and complaint. If this happens, you will be served with a summons and complaint showing the amount of the suit but the total demand will also include filing fees and attorney's cost, usually 25% of the balance you owe on your credit card account. Imagine that you think you already owe a lot of money but now your debt has increased by the amount of the lawyer's fee. That is why many lawyers think that the strategy of putting your account into litigation right away is a very effective collection tactic.

It is a fact of life that sadly, not all lawyers operate ethically---what a surprise! There are some who serve you with a summons and the complaint but wait for your response before actually filing the Complaint in court. This saves them the expense of actually filing the suit. There are some who file the Complaint in court but never actually serve you with the summons. This is called "sewer service", a practice of some lawyer's process servers to affirm delivery of legal documents to named defendants when in fact service had not been effectuated and in some cases not even attempted. Their intention is to obtain a default judgment against you, the defendant because you cannot possibly answer a Complaint you never received. If they succeed in obtaining a default judgment or a summary judgment, the situation will be harder to rectify. Imagine that you could have avoided the quagmire if you just wrote *The Letter* in the first place and replied to their settlement proposal. If it gets to this point, there are still some "do it yourself" simple legal procedures you can follow, discussed in Volume 2 to extricate yourself from the predicament you got yourself into. Creditors' collectors and other representatives must abide by the law. If they have a deficiency in their collection procedures or in their record keeping, their case against you can be thrown out---forever (dismissed with prejudice). I can allude to my own experience. I was surprised to find out that the credit card companies were unable to produce my credit card applications, the ones I filled out on paper application forms when I applied for their credit cards many years ago. Perhaps they have a poor or very limited storage capacity that compels them to discard these paper applications after several years. So, the likelihood is that they will not be able to produce your credit application if you ask them for a copy. Creditor's failure to retain such an important document and your creditor's failure to produce a copy when you ask them for it could just wipe out your alleged debt if you know how to use this against them. How can they sue you for "Breach of Contract" if they cannot prove the existence of a contract? This is further discussed in greater detail in Volume 2. If you want to have a little fun with a collector the next time one calls you, ask him or her a series of questions:

- "Who are you?
- Are you working for the creditor on contingency basis or did you buy my account from the creditor?
- If you are working for the creditor, can you show me proof that they've authorized you to collect on their behalf?
- If you bought the debt from the creditor, do you have a copy of the invoice showing terms of sale between you and the creditor?
- Can you provide proof that you are authorized to do business in my state?"

Then keep quiet and wait for the answer. Whatever the collector says at this point, just keep saying you will not discuss the matter until proof is provided and give him/her your email address so he can send proof. Don't hold your breath, though.

My Personal Experience

I owed over $100,000 in credit card debt but I was not poor. I had a steady job, owned my own house with only 8 years remaining on a 15-year mortgage, a fully paid Lexus, a few thousand dollars in a checking account and had a 401k account with a balance of over $80,000 invested in an assortment of mutual funds. I kept borrowing on my credit cards because I lost my job and the job I found after a one year job search only paid half of what I used to make. To make matters worse, two of my family members whom I am responsible for had health issues and the insurance deductibles and co-pays depleted our emergency fund. My credit card debt was hurting my life. I took cash advances from one credit card to pay another. I thought of borrowing some money from my sister to pay my minimum monthly payment, but I asked myself, "What will I do next month?" I was stressed out and had trouble sleeping just thinking how long my ever-increasing debt would continue to gnaw at me. I sat down in front of my computer and created an excel amortization schedule. If I only made the minimum payments and do not borrow anymore, with compounding interest of 25% APR, I will still owe a substantial amount of money after many years of minimum monthly payments. The interest alone that I will have paid would total close to $100,000. Filing for bankruptcy protection was not an option because the truth is I was not insolvent. I could have liquidated my assets, sold my house, paid my $100,000 debt and still be left with a small amount of cash after all is said and done. But with the medical problems my family members were having at that time, selling the house and uprooting the family would have been devastating. I did not want to touch my retirement fund prematurely, pay ordinary income tax rate on it plus the 10% IRS penalty, although I also gave that some thought and I could have easily done that to lighten the load. I thought that there has to be another option for credit card debtors like me who are (temporarily) going through some tough financial times. When times were good I made regular timely monthly payments, at least the minimum, but I've had a reversal of fortune. So while surfing the net, I came across lots of ads for free advice for credit card negotiation, credit card debt consolidation, debt forgiveness, debt settlement agencies and others. Since the information was advertised to be free, I took advantage and contacted many of them. The strategy of most debt consolidators and in particular the one I consulted is to get a reduction of the interest rates and negotiate a lower monthly payment. In return I will pay them a certain percentage of what they end up saving me. I did not like the numbers they presented me so I tried other freebies I found on the internet.

A debt settlement agency did not want to take my case on my terms, i.e. to negotiate at least an 85% reduction of my debts. The counsellor said they will spend a lot time negotiating with my creditors on my behalf because the creditors will not likely be receptive to negotiation of such a big reduction since I had a steady job and a large equity on my principal residence. According to the debt settlement counsellor, it is easy enough for the creditor to file suit, win a judgment and garnish my wages or put a lien on my house. They would have taken my case but on their own terms, i.e. to automatically take money from my checking account to put into their own savings account supposedly to use as bait for my creditors for negotiating a 50% reduction of my debts when the money grows to that target amount. Furthermore, part of their plan was to automatically take an additional 16% of my total debt out of my checking account as their non-refundable fee. Needless to say, I ran the other way.

One of the ads I saw was from an attorney specializing in credit card debt negotiation and he offers free consultation. His office was only 20 minutes away so I made an appointment to see him. I felt comfortable with the consultation and was impressed with the knowledge he seems to possess so I retained his services for a flat fee of $2000. He will not take my case on contingency basis, i.e. take a portion of what he saves as his fee. The best result I got from hiring him was that I had relief from the creditors for months. I simply gave his name and phone number to my creditors whenever a collector called or when one sent a letter. But after a year of what I thought were negotiations with my creditors, he happily informed me that he succeeded in negotiating a 20% reduction of what I owed meaning I am still on the hook for at least $80,000. It was a big disappointment so I did not accept the various offers. To make matters worse, months after I fired him he continued sending me bills for the time he spends in receiving, reading and forwarding creditors' reminders and collection letters to me.

It took another year of trial and error, of countless hours on the phone and writing meaningless letters, most of which I copied from various articles and websites in the internet before I saw the light at the end of the tunnel. None of the free advice and letters I found in the internet worked. I finally came up with *The Letter* that uniformly worked in negotiating down my debt with my credit card providers. After mailing *The Letter* to my creditors, I received a reply from a collection agency representing one of them offering to accept 50% of what I owed as full payment of my debt. But that was not good enough for me so I countered with 5%. We finally agreed on 10% of the original amount as full and final settlement of my balance. Considering I had not paid them for a year, I accumulated a little cash, so I was happy to grab the offer and pay in full. I had five credit cards with large balances and *The Letter* worked satisfactorily on four of the accounts. The last hold-out, surprisingly the account with the smallest balance at $13,000, chose to take me to arbitration. This negotiation-resistant creditor incorrectly perceived that they might collect more money from me that way but they were wrong. More of that in Volume 2. I settled the other 3 accounts for between 5% and 15%. It cost me a little more than $9,000 to settle the 4 accounts from the money I had saved by not making the large minimum monthly payments for almost a year and some from the money that I borrowed from my 401k account at 5% APR. I was surprised that not one creditor even referred to the contents of *The Letter*. Instead, they went right into negotiation mode to try to get as much money from me as they could. I thought the creditors will contest what I wrote on *The Letter*, but that did not happen.

Your Tax on Cancelled Debt

One thing to remember before it gets totally forgotten is that the creditors will send you an IRS Form 1099-C after the end of the year for the amount of money they forgave. This IRS form is also known as Cancellation of Debt Income (CODI) report. In my case, that was approximately $90,000. The creditors are supposed to send this form to the debtor with a copy to the IRS by February 28 of the year following the year of the cancellation of debt. The amount is taxable as ordinary earned income for the year shown on form 1099-C. My composite tax rate for federal and state income taxes was 25% for the year indicated which meant I owed an additional $22,500 for the cancelled debt. I found a legal loophole which is explained in Volume 2 of this series. See Chapter, "Do You Have to Pay Tax on Cancelled Debt?" https://www.amazon.com/dp/B01ACTBTIU/ref=rdr_kindle_ext_tmb Therefore, I have not yet paid the tax, but it has been over 7 years since my letter to the IRS disputing the 1099-C forms. I assume the statute of limitation has run out since I have not heard from the IRS again.

DO'S AND DONT'S of Credit Card Debt Negotiation

Here are some of the things I learned that I want to pass on to save you a lot of time and accomplish your goal of obtaining credit card forgiveness much quicker than I did:
- Don't waste your time negotiating by phone. If you call the credit card company's customer service number you will waste a lot of time waiting for an answer. From my experience, most of them are staffed by "call center" employees who may be operating in locations outside the United States. Decision makers in most cases are not in the same location. Generally, the first person you talk to will not know what to do and will have to refer your call to somebody else. When you finally speak to a supervisor, you have to explain yourself all over again and usually nothing will happen. They are required to type a short story of the conversation but the conversation can often be misinterpreted or deliberately twisted. It can take a long time to work your way up the system to get a concrete answer. They will tape your phone conversation and may use your words against you in a court of law.
- Do not deal with a debt consolidation company. You can do much better on your own. Besides, there are many that are fly-by-night organizations that are here today, gone tomorrow. Many of them have counselors who have very low qualifications. Some of these companies are outright scams.
- Do not hire a professional negotiator such as a debt settlement counselor or lawyer. My personal experience is that they did not do much better than me and their fees only ate into the much smaller amount they were proposing to save me. Some of them charge an hourly fee based on the time they spend on your case and some of them charge a percentage of the amount they save you. Some of them engage in unfair and deceptive

business practice. The tell-tale signs are, demanding money from you for their non-refundable fee before they even do any work and asking you to transfer a monthly allowance to their own savings account supposedly for settlement of your debts. Reputable companies, many of whom are non-profit organizations will set up an escrow account in your name for the purpose of setting up a savings account to be used to settle your debts. They should also provide a full disclosure of their fees and inform you of the negative impact debt negotiation will cause on your credit report.

-   Always send 2 copies of your letters. One by regular first class mail and one by certified mail, return receipt requested. Do not discuss nor accept any settlements by phone. Any agreement must be in writing.

-   After sending *The Letter*, do not be rattled if you do not receive a reply immediately. You may have to send several follow up letters. Just add this first paragraph*:* ***"I am once again resending this letter (for the second time, for the third time) by certified mail in the event the original was not received by the responsible person in your office and to make sure the ball is in your court. If I do not receive your reply within 10 days, I will assume that you have accepted my offer, closed my account and stopped adding interest and penalties to my account. If my assumption is incorrect, you must reply within 10 days of receipt of this letter."***

When the Credit Card Company Refuses to Negotiate

If you do not receive a reply after sending 3 follow up letters, you can assume that the creditor perceives they can get more money from you by prolonging the collection process which can eventually lead to their filing of a lawsuit against you. If they think you will resume your payments by threatening to file a complaint against you in court or through arbitration, they will not accept your proposal. You must take action before this negotiation-resistant creditor goes too far. A lawsuit puts you at a definite disadvantage. When a lawsuit is filed, you will have to answer the Complaint within the time prescribed by the Court and pay a filing fee. In many cases, a skilled lawyer will file a Motion for Summary Judgment against you after only a short period of filing the Complaint and most likely you won't know what to do on your own, so you will be forced to see a lawyer to draft an opposition to the plaintiff's Motion for Summary Judgment if you don't want the judgment to stick. See Volume 2 in this series on how to answer a Complaint and how to oppose a Plaintiff's Motion for Summary Judgment.

For the information of the reader, the definition of Default Judgment in the legal dictionary is: "Under rules of Civil Procedure, when a party against whom a judgment for affirmative relief is sought has failed to plead (i.e., answer) or otherwise defend, the party is in default and a judgment by default may be entered either by the clerk or the court". The definition of Summary Judgment in the legal dictionary is: "A procedural device used during civil litigation to promptly and expeditiously dispose of a case without a trial. It is used when there is no dispute as to the material facts of the case and a party is entitled to judgment as a Matter of Law".

You may be able to answer a Complaint on your own without an attorney, with the help of the internet, the court clerk or just by studying the rules of civil procedure on your state's website, but I doubt you have enough legal knowledge to oppose a Motion for Summary Judgment. A sample Opposition is included in Volume 2 of this series.

You can avoid all this by sending your creditor a "Validation of Debt, Cease and Desist Letter" immediately when it becomes apparent that the creditor refuses to negotiate reduction of your debt. Validation of Debt, Cease and Desist Letter is an important tool for the debtor and is fully discussed in more detail in Volume 2. A sample is shown below. There are many free samples of this letter in the internet but the one shown below should create a problem for the creditor or collector. It is unlikely that the creditor can produce all the requested information which means that they won't be able to validate the debt.

Validation of Debt, Cease and Desist Letter-Sample

By **FIRST CLASS AND CERTIFIED MAIL RETURN RECEIPT REQUESTED**

Date: xx/xx/xx
Name of Credit Card Company, Collection Company or Law Firm
Address

RE: Account No. xxxx xxxx xxxx $20,000

Dear Mr. or Ms. Xxxxxxx (It is important to address your letter to the responsible person who sent you the collection letter)
This is a REQUEST for validation of debts.

This letter is being sent in reply to your enclosed statement of account (or collection letter) dated xx/xx/xx a copy of which is attached.

Be advised that this is not a refusal to pay, but a notice sent pursuant to the Fair Debt Collection Practices Act, 15 USC 1692g Sec. 809 (b) that your claim is disputed and validation is requested. This is NOT a request for "verification" or proof of my mailing address, but a request for VALIDATION made pursuant to the above named Title and Section. I respectfully request that your offices provide me with competent evidence that I have any legal obligation to pay you.

Please provide me with the following:

-What the money you say I owe is for;

-Explain and show me how you calculated what you say I owe;
-Provide me with receipts of the charges that equal the amount you say I owe;
-Provide me with copies of any papers that show I agreed to pay what you say I owe;
-A Certified copy of my original credit application when I applied for your credit card;
-Provide a verification or copy of any judgment if applicable;
-Identify the original creditor if applicable;
-Prove the Statute of Limitations has not expired on this account;
-Show me that you are licensed to do business in my state. Provide your state license registration number and a copy of your certificate of good standing;
-Provide me with your Registered Agent's name and address.

At this time I will also inform you that if your offices have reported invalidated information to any of the 3 major Credit Bureau's (Equifax, Experian or TransUnion) this action might constitute fraud under both Federal and State Laws. Due to this fact, if any negative mark is found on any of my credit reports by your company or the company that you represent I will not hesitate in bringing legal action against you for the following:

Violation of the Fair Credit Reporting Act
Violation of the Fair Debt Collection Practices Act
Defamation of Character

If your offices are able to provide the proper documentation as requested in the aforementioned Declaration, I will require at least 30 days to investigate this information and during such time all collection activity must cease and desist. Also during this validation period, if any action is taken which could be considered detrimental to any of my credit reports, I will consult with my legal counsel for suit. This includes listing of any information to a credit reporting repository that could be inaccurate or invalidated or verifying an account as accurate when in fact there is no provided proof that it is.

If your offices fail to respond to this validation request within 30 days from the date of your receipt, all references to this account must be deleted and completely removed from my credit file and a copy of such deletion request shall be sent to me immediately.

This letter will serve as my written request that no telephone contact be made by your offices to my home or to my place of employment. Please be informed that my employer does not allow calls from collection agencies or creditors. If your offices attempt telephone communication with me, including but not limited to computer generated calls and calls or correspondence sent to or with any third parties, it will be considered harassment and I will have no choice but to file suit. All future communications with me MUST be done in writing and sent to the address noted in this letter by USPS certified mail return receipt requested. Also, please be reminded that each violation to my request to cease and desist carries a civil liability of $1000 for each occurrence in accordance with FDCPA, 15 USC 1692k Sec. 813. Be informed that I will document every violation by logging each call received from your offices.

It would be advisable that you assure that your records are in order before I am forced to take legal action. This is an attempt to correct your records, any information obtained shall be used for that purpose.

Sincerely,

**Card Holder's Signature
CARDHOLDER'S NAME
ADDRESS
CITY, STATE, ZIP
EMAILADDRESS: xxxxxx**

Cc: Original Creditor (Credit Card Company)
****

••

According to the FDCPA, the creditor must cease and desist collection efforts until they have duly validated your alleged debt. They must provide everything requested on your letter including and especially a certified copy of your original signed credit card application. A generic-computer generated card member agreement is not validation. Copies of 6 months' statements, which is probably what the creditor/collector will send you in answer to your request, do not constitute validation of debt. If this happens, write this follow up letter by certified mail:

****

"Dear Creditor or Collector (address your letter to a specific person):

Thank you for your letter dated xx/xx/xx, a copy of which is enclosed. Your letter includes copies of my statements for 6 months, a generic computer generated card member agreement and a printout showing my name and the date of my supposed credit card application. Please be informed that these documents and your reply does not fulfill your obligation for Validation of Debt under FDCPA 15 USC 1692g Sec. 809 (b). The following court case will provide you with guidance on your obligation to provide the required debt validation:

In LVNV Funding, L.L.C. v. Colvell, 421 N.J.Super. 1 (App. Div. 2011), the Appellate Division reversed the trial court's grant of summary judgment for the plaintiff because plaintiff failed to submit evidence sufficient to sustain its burden of proof. Colvell involved the claim of Plaintiff on an allegedly defaulted credit card account. The opinion of the Court read in part: "In particular, when suing to collect the balance allegedly owed on an unpaid revolving credit card account, the creditor must prove more than merely the total amount remaining unpaid. ...the creditor must set forth the previous balance, and identify all transactions and credits, as well as the periodic rates, the balance on which the finance charge is computed, other charges, if any, the closing date of the billing cycle, and the new balance."

Please provide all the documents requested in my Validation of Debt Letter dated xx/xx/xx which was received by your office on xx/xx/xx as per enclosed postal receipt. If any of the documents cannot be provided, please state the reason. Cease and desist collection of this alleged debt until you have duly validated the debt by providing the documents that I have requested.

Sincerely,

Card Holder's Signature
CARDHOLDER'S NAME
ADDRESS
CITY, STATE, ZIP
EMAILADDRESS: xxxxxxx
Cc: Original Creditor (Credit Card Company)

****

If the creditor or collection agency fails to validate the debt, then files a lawsuit against you, you can use their failure to validate the debt as one of your affirmative defenses in your answer to their complaint. This is discussed in more detail in volume 2 of this series. Another option is for you to file your own Defendant's Motion for Summary Judgment, i.e. as a matter of law they failed to validate your debt in accordance with the law, FDCPA 15 USC 1692g Sec. 809(b). This is also discussed in more detail in volume 2 of this series.

****

If the creditor or collection agency continues to send you collection letters, final notices, threats of lawsuits and letters threatening to destroy your credit, the following letter usually works. In my experience, after writing the letter that follows, they stop sending collection letters and I never hear from them again:

Via Certified Mail
Dear Credit Card Company:

I am required by law to send you this FINAL NOTICE before the filing of a lawsuit. The lawsuit will be for harassment, fraud and violation of the FDCPA, 15 USC 1692k, Sec. 813. Each separate violation of this section carries a penalty of $1000. Your enclosed collection letter/statement constitutes your first violation. There have been four other violations of the above-mentioned section for calls made into my home/office after you were notified to cease and desist.

Records will show that I mailed your company a **VALIDATION OF DEBT REQUEST** on xx-xx-xx which was received by Mr. Smith from your office on xx-xx-xx as per enclosed copy of the postal receipt. You failed to validate my alleged debt within the time required by law and the time within which to validate such debt has expired.

Please confirm that my account has a zero balance and that invalidated debt **WILL NOT** be reported to credit reporting agencies. Failure to respond to this letter and receipt of another collection letter/statement from you will compel me to file a civil suit against your company and the officers named below:

Mr. Peter Smith, Chairman of the Board
Mr. John Jones, Director

Please let me have your response within 10 days of receipt of this certified mail.

Sincerely,

Card Holder's Signature
CARDHOLDER'S NAME
ADDRESS
CITY, STATE, ZIP
EMAILADDRESS: xxxxxxx

****

Please note that the names mentioned are fictitious. You may find the real names of the officers of the credit card company by doing a google search. The above-mentioned letter usually works although some of them still reported my alleged invalidated debt to credit reporting agencies. If you experience the same, refer to the Chapter, "How to Mitigate Negative Credit Report" in the book, https://www.amazon.com/DEBT-FORGIVENESS-WHEN-CREDITORS-DECIDE-ebook/dp/B01ACTBTIU/ref=sr_1_5?s=digital-text&ie=UTF8&qid=1486240846&sr=1-5&keywords=Arthur V. Prosper#reader_B01ACTBTIU

WRITE THIS LETTER

DATE

CERTIFIED RETURN RECEIPT REQUESTED

CREDIT CARD COMPANY
ADDRESS
CITY, STATE, ZIP

ACCT NO. xxxxx xxxxx xxxxx – Statement Dated, xx/xx/xx
BALANCE, $40,000

Sir or Madam:

      First, this will serve as your authorization from me to close the above-mentioned account immediately. I have enclosed herewith the credit card associated with the account and cut in half for security reasons.

      The above-mentioned account is unverified and the balance shown is disputed. Therefore, be informed that I will no longer make any payments towards this unverified account.

      However, I am able to pay you as full and final payment, 5% of the above-mentioned balance, the amount of which is Two Thousand Dollars ($2,000.00). Should you accept this proposal, please sign the enclosed "Release" and I will send my check within 7 days of receipt of the fully executed "Release".

      If you choose to settle this matter in Court or through Arbitration, please include the following documents in your Complaint:

1. A certified copy of the signed credit card holder agreement, not a generic unsigned computer generated agreement.

2. Copies of any amendments to the alleged cardholder agreements that apply to this unverified account.
3. Proof that the alleged card holder received such amendments and assented to its terms.

Please let me have your acceptance of my proposal in writing within 30 days of receipt of this letter so that I can send the amount as proposed as full settlement of the balance. A lack of response to this letter will be regarded as your agreement to close my account and your agreement to stop adding interest, late fees and penalties to this account.

The enclosed "Release" will serve as our agreement for full settlement of the balance. Please sign it and return it to me at your earliest convenience and I will mail you my check immediately.

This communication is provided solely for the purpose of notifying you to communicate in writing only and does not constitute an acknowledgement of the alleged debt shown above. Please reply by email for a more expeditious resolution of this case.

Sincerely,
Card Holder's Signature
CARDHOLDER'S NAME
ADDRESS
CITY, STATE, ZIP
EMAILADDRESS: xxxxxx

The above letter gives the impression that you know something about collections and the legal process. This is one letter that a customer service clerk would bring to the attention of his/her supervisor immediately for decision. It is not one of those run of the mill letters that begs for mercy and talks of the misfortune that a credit card holder had encountered. As previously discussed, creditors but especially credit card companies are never merciful. They are in business to make money not to listen to your heartaches. If they think they can collect from you, they will keep pressing on. If they think, they will just spend a lot of time, money and resources going after you, they will bail out and abandon the case or settle for much less.

The original creditor/credit card provider must sign the "Release" if/when they agree with your proposal. The "Release" will serve as the "Settlement Agreement" so it should be attached to your letter for the convenience of the creditor. A sample is shown below.

Release - Sample

For and in consideration of the sum of Two Thousand Dollars ($2000.00), paid by ("Your Name"), Debtor to (Creditor/Credit Card Company's Name), Creditor, Creditor hereby fully and forever releases and discharges "Your Name" from any and all claims, complaints, causes of action, debts, sums of money, controversies, agreements, promises, damages and liabilities of any kind or nature whatsoever, whether accrued or unaccrued, liquidated or contingent, and now known or unknown, based on, related to, or arising from any event that has occurred before (Creditor/Credit Card Company's Name) signs this Release and based upon, related to or arising out of a certain credit card account of "Your Name", Number xxxx xxxx xxxx xxxx. Furthermore, (Creditor/Credit Card Company's Name) will consider this account, "Paid as Agreed".

(Creditor/Credit Card Company's Name) also forever waives, releases, discharges and gives up all claims, whether accrued or unaccrued, liquidated or contingent, real or perceived, and known or unknown, and all claims for breach of implied or express contract, breach of promise, breach of the covenant of good faith and fair dealing, misrepresentation, negligence, fraud, estoppel, violation of public policy, all claims for attorneys' fees or other fees or costs incurred for any reason.

This release is to be held in escrow until the payment of Two Thousand Dollars ($2000.00) is received by the Creditor/Releasor.

Releasor/Creditor _____
Releasor/Creditor's   Authorized   Representative
_____
Date _____

Counter Settlement Letter

If you receive the creditor's offer for a 50% discount which is probably what you will receive, write the following counter settlement letter:

DATE

CERTIFIED RETURN RECEIPT REQUESTED

CREDIT CARD COMPANY
ADDRESS
CITY, STATE, ZIP

ACCT NO. xxxxx xxxxx xxxxx – Statement Dated, xx/xx/xx
BALANCE, $40,000

Sir or Madam:

Reference is made to your letter dated xx/xx/xx a copy of which is attached. Thank you for your offer to accept a 50% settlement of my alleged balance. I can only pay $2000 at present. However, I may be able to borrow an additional $1000 from relatives within the next 10 days. If you accept my final offer of $3000 to settle my alleged debt of $40,000, please fill out and sign the enclosed "Release" and return it to me within the next 10 days. If I do not hear from you within 10 days, I will presume that you have accepted my offer, closed my account, stopped charging interest and that you will be sending me the "Release" in due time.

Thanks in advance for your kind consideration and cooperation. I am looking forward to your favorable response.

This communication is provided solely for the purpose of notifying you to communicate in writing only and does not constitute an acknowledgement of the alleged debt shown above.

Sincerely,
Card Holder's Signature
CARDHOLDER'S NAME
ADDRESS
CITY, STATE, ZIP
EMAILADDRESS: xxxxxx

****

If you receive another unacceptable offer you may counter again by increasing your offer in $500 increments up to 15% of the balance if you can afford it. Otherwise, if you have reached your limit, be firm with your final figure if that is all you can afford. But you get the idea that it is all negotiation at this point. Your creditor will probably accept a certain amount rather than go through the expense of suing you especially after you gave them the impression that you possess the time, skill and inclination to fight their lawsuit if they decide to take that route.

****

Recently, readers have been reporting that many credit card companies have been ignoring *The Letter* and are simply responding with a form letter like the one that follows:

Dear Credit Card Holder:
This letter is in response to your correspondence received regarding your account. We understand that borrowers may experience income reductions, financial difficulties or life changes that can affect their ability to make payments, but informing our office of your current financial situation does not release you from your contractual obligation

to pay in a timely manner. Please be assured that we want to work with you to determine an acceptable payment arrangement that works for all parties. Please contact Mary O. at (800) 555-1212, extension 69, or John T. at extension 96 to discuss options that may be available for the account.

Sincerely,
Credit Card Company

****

If you receive the above letter, please be aware that the creditor wants you to call them so they can record your conversation and get you to admit to your alleged debt and get you to agree to pay "a very small amount" each month. For example, if your minimum monthly payment is $1000 a month, they may reduce it to $500 and may also reduce your interest, say from 25% to 15% but you may have to continue paying for 10 years longer. If you find this acceptable, then *The Letter* worked for you and there is nothing wrong with accepting such an arrangement--- again if paying 15% APR for an additional 10 years is OK with you. As for me and for many other debtors, our objective as defined in this book is to negotiate a FULL and FINAL settlement of 5% to 15% of the balance. As in all negotiations, the two parties have different objectives. The creditor's objective is to come up with the biggest amount "they think" they can collect from me and I should be grateful that they are giving me any type of discount. My objective is to convince them that what I am offering (5% to 15%) is the most they can collect from me. If all fails and the credit card company completely ignores your settlement proposals, you must go to Step 6 of this process and write the creditor a "Validation of Debt, Cease and Desist Letter" as shown in the previous chapter. Also, please be aware that if you called them in response to their "nice letter" which appears on the surface, sympathetic to your financial difficulties or life changes, they may have recorded your conversation and got you to admit that you owe the money.

If you send them the "Validation of Debt Request", their response could be a transcript of your conversation wherein, in one way or another, you unwittingly admitted to your debt which may constitute "Validation of Debts" under the FDCPA. That is why it is important never to call them, but to request them to always communicate in writing. The credit card company will wait for at least 90 days or 3 or more missed monthly payments before taking it to the next level of more aggressive collection measures such as a "final notice", letter from a local attorney threatening lawsuit, etc. In summary, there is nothing to gain by calling the credit card company. You will be talking to "work-out clerks" who are not your friends and who have a script in front of them to get you to admit to your alleged debt and get you to agree to pay "a smaller monthly payment". Work-out clerks of a bank's loss mitigation department are very skilled when it comes to negotiating with you by phone. Unlike junk debt collectors, they will sound polite and sympathetic and they can get you to admit to your debt without you even knowing it. Their script provides them with plenty of leeway in getting you to pay a much smaller monthly payment. For example, if your minimum payment has risen to $950 a month, the clerk may offer you a declining amount until you say yes. The conversation may go this way: "I know you are really going through some financial hard times. We understand that. Can you afford to pay a minimum of $750 a month?" If you answer no, he/she may ask, "What is the minimum you can afford to pay". If you answer $100 per month, he/she may reply, "It's too low. My supervisor will never accept that". The two of you will keep up this back and forth negotiation until you stop and say, "that is really all I can afford". He/she will then say, "If that is the maximum you can afford to pay every month, let me get an approval from my supervisor". Then he/she may come back and say, "My supervisor says add another $50 and we have a deal". Or, "Good news. My supervisor approved your new monthly payment but if you miss one payment, your interest rate is going up to 35%. Do you agree? In some cases, the work-out clerk may send you another document that you will have to sign admitting to the balance of your account and a higher interest rate and promising to pay the much smaller monthly minimum you agreed to. If you sign it---shazam!!---the work-out clerk just validated your debt. That is why for me, there is nothing to gain by calling them.

Some companies are tougher than others. I have received reports that Discover, Citibank, TD Bank and Chase have been receptive to settlement offers. On the other hand, Amexco, Cap One and Bank of America have been known to be tougher and would rather hire tough collection law firms that will put your delinquent account into litigation immediately.

The following are a representation of the type of letters my readers received after sending *The Letter*. Certain confidential information was changed to protect the privacy of all concerned:

****

Credit Card Account No. xxxxxxxx, - BALANCE $14,500.00

Dear xxxxxxxx:

Your account status continues to remain delinquent and we want you to know that you are eligible to settle your account for $5,800.00 based on the current status of your account. You may pay the settlement amount in up to three monthly installments. However, you must call us to take advantage of this opportunity and to learn the settlement terms. Simply mailing in your payment will not result in an approved settlement. This opportunity is based on the current status of your account. If the status of your account changes (including your account balance), your eligibility for settlement will be determined at the time you call us.

BENEFITS OF SETTLING YOUR ACCOUNT

Here are a few benefits of settling your account as long as your payments are made on time:
- Collection calls will stop.
- Once the settlement is approved interest and late fee charges will stop.
- If you pay the full settlement amount when due, we will report the balance of your account to credit bureaus as zero but paid less than the total amount owed.

To discuss this settlement offer on your account or other options that you may qualify for, please call us today at 1-866-974-1372. If this does not meet your needs, we can also discuss other options which may be available to you. Please call us today to prevent your account from becoming more delinquent. We're not obligated to renew this offer, however opportunities to settle may be available at a later date.

Please call today so we can work together to find a solution.
Sincerely,
G. Jones
VP Credit Card Division
ABC BANK

****

XYZ Credit Card Company will help you save. Your account is eligible for a settlement. Call 1-866-374-1352
OUTSTANDING BALANCE: $9,207.36
YOUR SETTLEMENT AMOUNT, BASED ON YOUR CURRENT BALANCE IS: $3,068.82
YOU SAVE: $6,134.54
To discuss this opportunity you must call us at 1-866-374-1352 by 11/15/2017.

Dear Credit Card Member:

Do not let this great opportunity pass. We noticed you have fallen behind in your payments and want you to know that you are eligible to settle your account for $3,068.82, based on the current status of your account, including your current balance. Please call 1-866-374-1352 to take advantage of this settlement offer or to find out about other ways we may be able to help you. If we do not hear from you by 12/15/2017, your account will charge off unless we either receive at least the minimum payment due reflected on your most recent statement by the payment due date, or you make other acceptable payment arrangements with us by that date. In the event your account charges off you will remain liable for the entire outstanding balance on your account and your account may be referred to a collection agency or attorney.

We've been able to help other card members and we would like to help you too. We would be happy to discuss whether we can offer other solutions that may be available to you, but there no time to waste, and taking care of this will never be any easier than it is right now.

We hope you will call us today at 1-866-374-1352 so we can work on this together and put it behind us.

**Sincerely,
T. Smith
VP Credit Card Division
XYZ BANK**

****

After my readers received the aforementioned settlement offers, they did not call the CC Companies. They mailed the counter-settlement letters by certified mail instead, after which a representative of the cc company negotiated back and forth with my readers by email until they agreed to a settlement amount.

Creditors' request for financial information

It has come to my attention that some of my readers recently received replies from their creditors who are indicating willingness to negotiate and forgive a large portion of the debt but are requesting the debtor to fill out a balance sheet, statement of net worth or cash flow projection. If you receive such a request my advice is NOT to fill out any of the forms but instead write the letter below:

****

Date: _____
Creditor's Name
Address

RE: Credit Card # xxxx-xxxx-xxxx-xxxx Balance: $40,000.
Dear Creditor:
Thank you for your reply to my request of forgiveness of my alleged debt.
Respectfully and regretfully, I will not be filling out a statement of net worth which you are requesting. As you know, credit card debt is unsecured and the credit line you provided when you opened my account was not based on my net worth but on my credit scores acquired from credit reporting agencies. With respect, your request for financial information long after credit was granted is unfair business practice and I will not provide it. I reiterate my offer of $2000 as full and final settlement of my alleged debt. If you fill out and return the enclosed "Release", I will immediately send you my check for $2000. If I do not hear from you within 10 days of receipt of this letter to the contrary, I will assume that you have accepted my offer of $2000 as full and final settlement of my alleged debt and that you will send me the "Release" in due time.

Respectfully,
Card Holder's Signature
CARDHOLDER'S NAME
ADDRESS
CITY, STATE, ZIP
EMAILADDRESS: xxxxxxx

****

A request for financial information by the creditor at this point is not a reasonable request. The information may be used against you in a court of law. They may lure you into a false sense of security to make you believe that their intention to negotiate at this point is amicable, fair and honest but beware. There is nothing friendly about debt collections and collectors will use every trick in the book to collect the most they can collect from you. Good debt collectors have learned not to take their job personally. Rather, they see themselves as soldiers in a battlefield, you as the enemy. They have a job to do and will employ quasi military strategy and tactics to collect. Your job is to dodge the bullets. Clearly, asking you to fill out a net worth statement is one of their tactics. Learning about your finances especially your bank balances, bank account numbers and assets you own or have interest in will only benefit them. So pretend you are Alexander the Great, stand your ground, with an impenetrable phalanx in front to protect you. Keep telling the enemy that what you say you can afford to pay is what they should accept as full settlement. Yes you may bargain and offer a maximum of $6000 (15%) as your final settlement offer if you have the money in cash so as to get rid of a $40,000 debt forever.

Sample timeline of the collection process

1/31/16 DEBTOR'S ACTION
Stops making payments and mails *The Letter* offering to settle balance for 5% of total. Debtor should not make any payments after this date unless it is the full settlement amount agreed to by creditor and debtor. Any partial payments will reset the statute of limitation clock. Debtor should save as much money as possible from this point on in the event of an acceptable counter-offer which may have to be paid in a lump-sum.

2/28/16 CREDITOR'S ACTION
Acknowledges receipt of letter and advises debtor to call customer service or a designated representative.

3/10/16 DEBTOR'S ACTION
Does not call creditor. Writes 2nd negotiation letter (counter-settlement letter). As a precaution, debtor and spouse close their checking and savings accounts at the bank that issued their credit card to prevent the bank from charging their accounts for "bad debt offset debit". See Volume 2, Chapter ". The Bank can Freeze Your Checking and Savings Accounts".

3/31/16 CREDITOR'S ACTION
  1. Accepts the offer or presents a counter-offer.

  2. Closes account but collection efforts intensify, urges debtor to make small payments, ignores debtor's settlement offer.

4/15/16 DEBTOR'S ACTION
  1. Accepts or rejects counter-offer, if any.

2. Since no reply to offer of settlement, debtor writes "Request for Validation of Debt, Cease and Desist Letter", sends letter by certified mail, return receipt requested.

5/31/16 CREDITOR'S ACTION
As a reply to "Request for Validation", sends debtor copies of statements or a print-out showing the dates when and how debtor applied for the credit card, last payment and last charge. May also include a generic unsigned computer generated card member agreement.

6/10/16 DEBTOR'S ACTION
Writes letter indicating Creditor has not validated debt in accordance with the FDCPA. See Volume 3/LETTERS, Debtor's Response to Creditor's Validation of Debt.

7/20/16 CREDITOR'S ACTION
1. Finally, accepts settlement offer or presents counter-offer.

2. Refers account to a local attorney.

7/31/16 DEBTOR'S ACTION
1. Pays settlement offer.

2. Receives final notice from attorney threatening lawsuit. Debtor writes letter informing attorney that his client, the CC company failed to validate debt. See, Volume 3/Letters.

8/20/16 CREDITOR'S ACTION
1. Attorney provides additional paperwork supposedly satisfying validation of debt clause.

2. Aggressive attorney ignores debtor's letter and sends debtor an unfiled Complaint (see sample Complaints in Debt Forgiveness Volume2 and Summons) thinking that debtor will

be intimidated into paying the balance upon receipt of legal papers.

9/15/16 DEBTOR'S ACTION
1. Ignores attorney's proof since time for validation has expired.

2. Waits for the service of the Summons, Replies to lawsuit (see sample Answer to Complaint in Volume 2) within the time prescribed by the court. Sends Request for Admissions, Interrogatories and Request for Production of Documents along with the Answer to Complaint. See, Volume 3/ Defendant Discovery.

10/31/16 CREDITOR'S ACTION
1. Creditor writes off balance and reports account to credit bureaus as "Charge Off". Sells account to junk debt collector. You will realize the debt was sold because the collection letter comes from a new collection agency and it may say, "This debt is now owned by XYZ Collection Agency".

2. Creditor's attorney decides it is too time consuming to reply to Defendant's Discovery so, ignores Discovery and Files a "Motion for Summary Judgment" instead. But in my experience and in the experience of over 100 of my readers, the Collector/attorney gives up at this point since it would be too time consuming to continue the case.

3. Court sets hearing date or assigns the case for mandatory in-person or telephone mediation.

11/20/16 DEBTOR'S ACTION
1. Great progress, no action needed until you hear again from the junk debt collector.

2. Opposes Plaintiff's Motion for Summary Judgment. See Volume 3/ Defendant's Opposition to Summary Judgment.

3. Writes the Court for an adjournment of hearing or mediation until discovery is completed. See Volume 3/Letters. Your objective is not to appear in court or participate in any mediation. The CC Company's attorney will have an advantage in a personal hearing or mediation since this is what he does for a living. He goes to court regularly and knows the mediators.

11/30/16 CREDITOR'S ACTION
1. Junk debt collector sends dunning letters and makes annoying daily collections calls.

2. Receives Defendant's Opposition to Motion, realizes this is not an easy case, calls debtor, accepts a lesser amount.

3. (a) Court adjourns case till discovery is complete.

3. (b) Court and/or Plaintiff rejects your adjournment request, compels both parties to a hearing or mediation even if discoveries of both parties have not been completed. Some jurisdictions require a personal appearance in Court for the hearing in which the judge may call for mediation before hearing the case. Some jurisdictions allow a phone mediation with a mediator agreed to by both parties. See Volume 3/How the Mediation Process Works.

12/10/16 DEBTOR'S ACTION
1. Ignores junk debt collector's collection efforts until collector threatens legal action.

2. Tells collection attorney by phone to present offer by email and to communicate by email only to avoid any

misunderstanding verbal communication may cause. Accepts or rejects offer. In case of rejection, writes Rejection of Settlement Offer#1, Volume3/Letters.

3. (a) At this point, Plaintiff usually gives up. Wait for the attorney's next move. See No. 2 if attorney calls to offer settlement. If attorney replies to your Discoveries, most likely, the answers were prepared by an office clerk who used a template. In most cases, an attorney will not even have time to review the answers. Most of the time their canned answers will begin with "Objection....xxxxxx", followed by a combination of the following: "defendant's request is irrelevant, compound, vague, uses terms not defined, subject to the attorney-client privilege, overly broad, burdensome, not likely to lead to discovery of admissible evidence, calls for a legal conclusion, etc. etc. etc." If they had gone as far as replying to your Discoveries, it is almost guaranteed that you will receive Plaintiff to Defendant Discoveries. They are hoping you will not answer their Discoveries which opens up the door for them to apply for a default judgment or court sanctions. They will not spend time replying to your Discoveries if they do not foresee the end game going their way. See Volume 3/How to Answer Plaintiff's Discoveries. Once they receive your reply to their Discoveries, they will quickly realize the futility of continuing the case and will quickly accept whatever you are offering.

3. (b) You must try to find a way to avoid a personal appearance in Court because your adversary can take advantage of you. Some reasons you can give the Court to request postponement of hearing, but which may be rejected, are: sickness or medical condition, taking care of a child, elderly or disabled. Being compelled to make a personal appearance for a hearing or mediation is the worst outcome you can expect. I myself and over 100 of my readers have avoided having to make personal court appearances by using the tactics in these books. But if you

must appear in court for a hearing, review Volume 2, Chapter "What Really Happens After Creditor Files Suit"

12/20/16 CREDITOR'S ACTION
1. Junk debt collector may continue annoying collection efforts but filing suit is unlikely.

2. Accepts offer from debtor.

3. (a) Does not make a move, case becomes dormant. In some jurisdictions, case may be dismissed with or without prejudice due to lack of prosecution. Or, receives debtor's answers to Plaintiff to Defendant Discoveries and creditor's attorney is forced to take a lower settlement because Defendant's answers will show Plaintiff that the cost to them will outweigh the benefit.

3. (b) Attorney's personal appearance gives him the upper hand since this is what he does for a living. See Volume 2/Chapter "What Really Happens After Creditor Files Suit". There are various scenarios in this chapter that will help you deal with the credit card company's attorney when you meet him in person.

12/20/16 DEBTOR'S ACTION
1. Do nothing

2. Congratulations

3. (a) congratulations

3. (b) If you have gone this far, this is do or die, the end of the rope. If you are a fighter, able to follow my strategy in Volume 2, and do not let yourself get intimidated by the attorney, you will come out well, perhaps getting a settlement of 5 to 15% of the claim. If your inclination is to

appear in Court, admit to your debt and beg for mercy, then you already lost. If you get scared and the attorney gets you to admit to the alleged debt without regard for the law that is there to protect consumers like you, the attorney may win a judgment against you not only for the principal but for additional legal fees. This is the way the attorney will intimidate or trick you into admitting you owe the money: "Hey, we both know you owe the money, let's just put this to bed so we can go home. When can you pay us?" Or "When can you pay the balance of your account? Can you agree to pay by installment if I write up the agreement now?" Bottom line: The attorney is representing his client, the big credit card company. However, he personally does not know if you really owe the money. But he has to take their side. If he has to follow the law, even he knows he has no leg to stand on. See Volume 2 as a guide on how you should deal with the creditor's attorney when you meet him face to face.

1/15/17 CREDITOR'S ACTION
3 (b) If you lose and were convinced by the attorney and mediator to sign an installment agreement, this agreement is sanctioned by the court and is as good as a judgment against you. You must pay in accordance with the agreement. Otherwise, the attorney can file a lien against your assets and/or writ of garnishment against your wages and soon the Sheriff may be knocking at your door.

4. If you are a fighter and do not get scared easily even by this big bad attorney wearing a thousand dollar suit and a strong cologne, with the mediator by his side, who looks like he might be thinking that you are a deadbeat, liar and a cheat, you will reject their proposal of admitting to your debt and the case will have to go to the judge for a hearing, most likely that same day. Or the judge may set a date for a trial another day if he thinks the Plaintiff has a case. If it goes that far, the lawyer will settle with

you rather than go through a full blown trial that he knows he will lose. It's true you are not a lawyer. But this much you should know, that on Complaints for Breach of Contract, the Plaintiff carries the burden of proving the existence of a contract. His best bet is for you to admit the existence of a contract. If you refuse to give in and admit it, he has the burden of producing the evidence to support his Complaint. On Complaints of "Account Stated", the plaintiff has to prove that, 1) he mailed you a statement of account, 2) you received the statement, 3) you kept the statement for an unreasonable amount of time without disputing the balance.

CONCLUSION-Volume 1

If you succeed in getting your debts forgiven, cancelled or reduced, do not feel bad for the Credit Card Company or think of yourself as a "bad guy", deadbeat or worse, a thief. Think of what just happened as a business transaction. If a manufacturer sells its products to a retailer on credit and the retailer cannot pay its debts anymore due to cash flow problems, that is just normal business, the free market economy turning its wheels. Rarely would the creditor consider its customer a thief, a liar or a bad guy. When you applied for a credit card, I am sure you had every intention of paying them back. Stop yourself from thinking that what you've accomplished is illegal, immoral or unethical. Credit card companies are not the embodiment of morality---far from it. You are simply using the same rules these credit card companies are using. They expect a certain number of accounts to default and you are one of a very few. Trust me there aren't that many accounts in default as a percentage of the whole or our banking system would collapse. Their deplorable interest rates, late fees and other transaction charges more than make up for the "few" accounts they have to devalue or write off. When you find yourself between a rock and a hard place, all you can do is choose the less painful of the two options and for me that is to take the hard line and tell my creditors to take my settlement offer or sue me----but if they sue me, they will lose. I am not proud of defaulting on my credit card debts, but my family comes first. Think about it, if no one ever defaults and the credit card companies have zero bad debts to write off, they will still charge us 13% to 35% interest rates. We will not get a letter from them next month saying, "We really had a good month of no bad debt write offs. Your interest rate is going down to 8%". It is like the government. You will not get a tax refund if the United States reduces its aid to Israel by $5 billion.

In 2009, the government bailed out the banks and other financial institutions to the tune of over a trillion dollars in taxpayer's money. These "too big to fail" institutions which own most of the credit card companies routinely change rules in the middle of the game, and all they have to do is send us notices that they know we will not read. Except for Lehman Brothers, Bear Stearns and a few smaller financial institutions, the shareholders of many of these "too big to fail" banks, investment companies and financial institutions did not lose a penny during the financial crisis. On the contrary the value of their stocks kept going up since the bottom of the bear market after the great recession of 2007-2009. The money that the banks will lose on your account for cancelling a portion of your debt is built into their profit margin. They borrow at 1% interest and they lend at 25%, what a margin! That is why the banking industry's CEOs and other officers are some of the highest paid professionals in the land. So think of your relationship with the credit card company as a business partnership. However, this business partner, the credit card company, has taken undue advantage of you over the years. Their Credit Card Member Agreement is so one-sided in their favor that if you read every page of the 30-page agreement, you probably won't sign it. But they did not need your signature because you agreed to their terms the moment you used their credit card (so they would claim). Think of the many notices they send you, written in fine print, which no one ever reads, that increase your interest rates, late fees, impose over-limit charges, reduce your grace period, institute stricter monitoring of your credit scores and make you sign away certain rights you may have under the law. They take the position that you have agreed to the changes inasmuch as they never received any objection from you. Think of the time when they gave you a supposed interest free cash advance and then you made a purchase which carries an interest rate of 25%. If you ask them to apply your next payment to the purchase to avoid paying the 25% interest longer, they will refuse and apply it to the cash advance that has zero interest so that they can keep collecting interest of 25% on the purchase. Is that fair? Think of the time you received an offer in the mail from them offering an interest free cash advance with a 5% service fee. Is that really interest free? Some of these tactics are outright unfair and deceptive, behavior that you do not expect from a reasonable and fair business partner but a scam artist trying to pull one over on you. So do not feel bad for the credit card companies.

As a conclusion to this conclusion, read this heart-rending reply from READER TWO who is answering READER ONE'S comment in the "Amazon Customer Reviews" section for this book. READER TWO makes a compelling argument. I can only hope that this book helped **READER TWO**:

READER ONE: ...instead of having to go through all of this nonsense because you're trying to get out of being responsible, why not agree to pay what you owe? Creditors are much more cooperative with people who actually have the desire to pay (at least SOMETHING) than those who just want to be excused from paying their debts. Grow up.

READER TWO: Grow up? How about this for growing up--a single mom of 3 working 60-70 hours per week, a house flood that caused over $30,000 in damage that the insurance refused to pay for, a son diagnosed with a brain lesion requiring immediate and very expensive neurosurgery, a ruptured water main costing several thousand dollars to repair after leaving us with no house water for 3 days, and a sister who abruptly became homeless and required financial support to survive for 6 months. All of this within an 8 month period and I still have ongoing medical expenses for a son with neuro issues. Want to guess how much my creditors care about any of this? How "cooperative" they have been? I suggest you grow up and come to the real world where most of the "reputable" creditors I have dealt with would prefer I let my son die rather than forgo a single late payment fee or a penny of that increased interest rate. This is not "nonsense." Most people turning to books such as this are far from irresponsible. In fact, most of the folks I've come across who are looking into solutions such as this are well aware their first and primary responsibility is to the health and welfare of their family/children and they have become desperate enough to attempt any solution they possibly can in order to see to that responsibility---this after overtime, second jobs, selling off all possible household goods and every other measure short of bank robbery have failed because the interest rates and late fees are increasing the debt at an accelerating rate, ballooning a once-manageable debt load into a ludicrous and completely impossible to pay tidal wave. Once one is at that point, one starts consulting bankruptcy lawyers out of sheer desperation, only to find that, because one has equity on one's house and has desperately been doing overtime in order to stay afloat, the bankruptcy payments would also be far too high to sustain for the required 5 years. So why not sell the house and use the equity to pay the bills? Well, because there isn't even half as much equity as there are bills, particularly after closing costs and capital gains taxes, and the cost of rent a small apartment is slightly more than the mortgage payment, leaving one in an even worse position in a very short amount of time. Not that the bill collectors aren't attempting to take the house anyway. And they haven't even gotten to garnishing wages yet. I'm sure it's coming. Welcome to the real world. This is the definition of grown up. Please, continue to blindly pass judgment on others. I'm sure it makes you feel very good about yourself.

*****<u>**End of Volume 1**</u>*****

If you have a tax deferred retirement plan, an IRA, a 401k, 403b or 457b and your money is invested in the stock market, are you prepared to lose 30 to 60% of your money when the market crashes? It is not a question of "if" but "when". It is guaranteed the stock market will crash when the next recession arrives, but when will that be? Learn more. Click on the link below:

SIMPLEST PATH TO WEALTH
https://www.amazon.com/Simplest-Path-Wealth-Turn-Million-ebook/dp/B01KPQB0OS/ref=asap_bc?ie=UTF8

VOLUME 2 INCLUDES:
-Validation of Debt, Cease and Desist Letter (A collector's worst nightmare)
-When Creditor Ignores Validation of Debt Letter
-Refusal of Arbitration
-How to answer a summons and Complaint
-Request for Production of Documents – Sample
-Plaintiff's Motion for Summary Judgment – (Defendant's Worst Nightmare)
-Defendant's Opposition to Plaintiff's Motion
-Letter to challenge IRS Form 1099-C, Cancellation of Debt Income (CoDI)
-How to mitigate negative marks on your credit report

****

Learn more about the subjects below from the author's new book:

https://www.amazon.com/Living-Rich-Loving-healthy-balanced-ebook/dp/B01GORIB4Y/ref=sr_1_3?s=digital-text&ie=UTF8&qid=1471625403&sr=1-3&keywords=Arthur V. Prosper

Living Rich and Loving It:
Your Guide to a Rich, Happy, Healthy, Simple and Balanced Life

o **Find a job you love** – If you cannot wait to get up and get to work every morning, then you have found the job you love. Otherwise, you need to read this chapter and the chapter, "Increase Your Income with these Ideas".

o **Personal Insurance** – Which is better, whole life or term insurance? How much insurance do you need? The answer may surprise you.

o **Annuities, what are they?**

o **Budgeting made easy** - Follow the sample and simple budget in the book and you will always have a monthly surplus.

o **Never buy Veblen Goods** – the savings will amaze you.

- Shop around for everything – if you are struggling to make ends meet, this chapter will show you why. Learn how to save more and spend less.

- How to purchase your primary residence – Pros and cons of owning vs. renting. The analysis chart shows the clear winner which will surprise you.

- Good debt, bad debt – when borrowing makes sense. Analysis table proves that some debts are good.

- Do Not Take Unnecessary Risks, Don't Do Anything Stupid – this chapter shows that stupidity is the great equalizer in life. Doing any of the things on the list may change your life or worse may end it in the blink of an eye.

- Never invest in a rental property – this chapter tells you why it is not worth being an absentee landlord.

- Never keep an emergency fund – the analysis chart shows you why and the answer will astound you.

- No Double Taxation on 401k Loans – never ever listen to Suze Orman that 401k loans are taxed twice.

- Planning for College – how to fund your children's college education. Read the many different ideas in this chapter which includes the availability of financial aid packages. The chart shows which colleges to choose and guides you towards a prudent decision.

- Increase Your Income - Make more money in your spare time with these ideas. When you read the money-making ideas in this chapter, you will scratch your head and say, "why didn't I think of that?"

o	**Create a Document Storage and Retrieval System** – So simple yet so effective. It will free up a lot of your limited living space.

o	**Stress-Free Personal Time Management** – This system will organize your day and free up plenty of your time for use at your leisure.

o	**How to Store and Safeguard Passwords** – Simple trick will help you create and remember strong passwords.

o	**How to maximize your Social Security benefits** – In light of the elimination of "File and Suspend" and "Restricted Application" strategies, the chart shows claiming strategies for 1) Single never married, 2) currently married, 3) married at least 10 years, divorced at least 2 years, currently single, 4) divorced, has remarried and currently married, 5) widow/widower, 6) surviving divorced spouse, married at least 10 years, currently single or remarried after the age of 60.

o	**Best places for retirement** – Some of these retirement communities are surprising. Some viable locations have ½ the cost of living of most cities in the U.S.

o	**Paying for Nursing Home and Long-Term Care**

o	**How to qualify for Medicaid benefits for LTC**

o	**How to reduce income to qualify for Medicaid**

- **How to reduce assets to qualify for Medicaid.**

- **Estate Planning – How to protect your estate from estate tax and inheritance tax.**

- **Enrich Your Life by Exploring the World – Travel as soon as you can while you are still young. This chapter discusses why the money you spend traveling and exploring the world is money well spent.**

- **Staying Healthy and Fit as You Age – There are a few minor behavior modification changes that you can put into practice that will keep you healthy throughout your retirement years.**

- **Live a Rich, Happy, Healthy, Simple and Balanced Life**

- **Learn more, click on the link below:** https://www.amazon.com/Living-Rich-Loving-healthy-balanced-ebook/dp/B01GORIB4Y/ref=pd_sim_sbs_351_2?ie=UTF8&psc=1&refRID=825N2SZCEYGWC1STH495

****

More about the Author

Arthur V. Prosper heads the finance department of a privately held manufacturing firm in the great state of New Jersey. Previously, he was the Vice President of Finance of the Kuoni Group and the Accounting Director of Cantel Medical. He was responsible for the financial objectives, retirement and benefit plans, investment goals and capital structures of the companies he worked for.

Supplemental Disclaimer

The use of the methods discussed in this book will likely adversely affect your credit worthiness and may result in you being subject to collections or being sued by creditors or collectors and may increase the outstanding balances of the amounts you owe prior to using the methods discussed herein. We do not guarantee that your debts will be resolved for a specific amount or percentage or within a specific period of time. Please contact a tax professional to discuss potential tax consequences of debt forgiveness.

The information contained in this book is provided to you "AS IS" and does not constitute legal advice. We make no claims, promises or guarantees about the accuracy, completeness, or any specific result from the use of the contents or adequacy of the information contained in this book. Information contained in this book should not be used as substitute for obtaining legal advice from an attorney licensed or authorized to practice in your jurisdiction. The author and publisher and their affiliates, parents, subsidiaries, assigns, officers, directors, shareholders, employees, representatives, agents and servants assume no responsibility to any person who relies on information contained herein and disclaim all liability in respect to such information.

Copyright and Trademark Ownership

Please be aware that any unauthorized use of the contents contained herein violates copyright laws, trademark laws, the laws of privacy and publicity, and/or other regulations and statutes. All text, images and other materials provided herein are owned by **Arthur V. Prosper** unless otherwise attributed to third parties. None of the content on these materials may be copied, reproduced, distributed, downloaded, displayed, or transmitted in any form without the prior written permission of **Arthur V. Prosper**, the legal copyright owner. However, you may copy, reproduce, distribute, download, display, or transmit the content of the materials for personal, non-commercial use provided that full attribution and citation to **Arthur V. Prosper** is included and the content is not modified, and you retain all copyright and other proprietary notices contained in the content. The permission stated above is automatically rescinded if you breach any of these terms or conditions. If permission is rescinded or denied, you must immediately destroy any downloaded and/or printed content.

****

PUBLISHER: A-TEAM, LP
PUBLISHER'S CATALOG:

DEBT FORGIVENESS Volume 2 WHEN CREDITORS DECIDE TO SUE: Erase Your Credit Card Debts
https://www.amazon.com/DEBT-FORGIVENESS-WHEN-CREDITORS-DECIDE-ebook/dp/B01ACTBTIU/ref=pd_sim_351_1?_encoding=UTF8&pd_rd_i=B01ACTBTIU&pd_rd_r=A001FFR7YYMRE7EEJ7T3&pd_rd_w=lDdkz&pd_rd_wg=W1P4U&psc=1&refRID=A001FFR7YYMRE7EEJ7T3

The Simplest Path to Wealth – Turn $50,000 into $3.3 Million
https://www.amazon.com/Simplest-Path-Wealth-Turn-Million-ebook/dp/B01KPQB0OS/ref=asap_bc?ie=UTF8

The Six Million Dollar Retiree: Your roadmap to a six million dollar retirement nest egg
https://www.amazon.com/Six-Million-Dollar-Retiree-retirement-ebook/dp/B073XTL47J/ref=sr_1_4?s=digital-text&ie=UTF8&qid=1504026864&sr=1-4&keywords=Arthur_V._Prosper

Dynamic Budgeting Techniques: Cut your expenses in half and double your income
https://www.amazon.com/Dynamic-Budgeting-Techniques-expenses-double-ebook/dp/B01LZA9O3W/ref=asap_bc?ie=UTF8

Living Rich & Loving It: Your guide to a rich, happy, healthy, simple and balanced life
https://www.amazon.com/Living-Rich-Loving-healthy-balanced-ebook/dp/B01GORIB4Y/ref=sr_1_3?s=digital-text&ie=UTF8&qid=1480539481&sr=1-3&keywords=Arthur_V._Prosper

www.ingramcontent.com/pod-product-compliance
Lightning Source LLC
Chambersburg PA
CBHW020453220526
45464CB00002B/973